MW01196408

"As a marriage aɪ been looking for for years. As Melissa so wisely says, singleness is not a stage, phase, or season. Most of all, singleness is not a problem to be solved but a route to togetherness. With the wisdom of a trustworthy guide and the care and humor of your best friend, Melissa offers inspiration, deep theological truth, and practical steps we all need to grow in community! The church and the broader culture need this message, and Melissa Zaldivar was absolutely the person to write it. Join me in underlining the whole thing!"

Nicole Zasowski, licensed marriage and family therapist and author of *What If It's Wonderful?*

"One of Melissa's superpowers is to see people who others sometimes overlook, and that's what she's done in this book. Singles will find a wise, compassionate friend in the pages of *Get Over Here,* and we're all the better for it."

Katy Boatman, cohost of the Single Purpose League community

"The beautiful approach to *Get Over Here* is found in the pages of Melissa Zaldivar's own story: never being defined by singleness, yet not shying away from the realities of it. This wise and measured guidebook will help every reader who is single feel seen, known, and understood right where they are."

Lisa Whittle, Bible teacher and bestselling author of *Jesus Over Everything*

"It is easy to be drawn in by Melissa's conversational humor, but what is so essential about this book is the way she sees what often goes unnoticed. The contours of community for friends who are single and sometimes struggling to fit in are named in this book. It's a hopeful encouragement for people who need to know they're not alone."

Sandra McCracken, singer-songwriter and author

"I know few women as adept at cultivating deeply satisfying community as Melissa Zaldivar. When she says, 'Get over here!' you'll want to be the first to show up."

Clarissa Moll, author and producer of
Christianity Today's *The Bulletin*

Get Over Here

Get Over Here

a single's guide to building meaningful community

Melissa Zaldivar

Revell

a division of Baker Publishing Group
Grand Rapids, Michigan

Published by Revell
a division of Baker Publishing Group
Grand Rapids, Michigan
RevellBooks.com

Printed in the United States of America

Library of Congress Cataloging-in-Publication Data
Names: Zaldivar, Melissa, author.
Title: Get over here : a single's guide to building meaningful community / Melissa Zaldivar.
Description: Grand Rapids, Michigan : Revell, a division of Baker Publishing Group, [2025] | Includes bibliographical references.
Identifiers: LCCN 2024053862 | ISBN 9780800746605 (paperback) | ISBN 9780800747176 (casebound) | ISBN 9781493450695 (ebook)
Subjects: LCSH: Single people—Religious life. | Single people—Conduct of life. | Communities—Religious aspects—Christianity.
Classification: LCC BV4596.S5 Z35 2025 | DDC 248.8086/52—dc23/eng/20250216
LC record available at https://lccn.loc.gov/2024053862

Cover design by Lindy Kasler

The author is represented by the literary agency of Wolgemuth & Wilson.

Baker Publishing Group publications use paper produced from sustainable forestry practices and postconsumer waste whenever possible.

25 26 27 28 29 30 31   7 6 5 4 3 2 1

— *To* —

Berean Bible Fellowship in Atascadero, California

Holy Trinity Church in Chicago, Illinois

Christ Church of Austin, Texas

Christ the King in Fayetteville, Arkansas

St. Mary's of Bethany in Nashville, Tennessee

North Shore Community Baptist Church in
Beverly, Massachusetts

———

*Thank you for always having room in the pew and
around the table for single brothers and sisters.*

Contents

· · · ·

Foreword by Lore Ferguson Wilbert 11

Introduction: The State of the Union 15

one Companionship 33

two Commiseration 53

three Connection 69

four Commitment 91

five Communication 107

six Consistency 127

seven Closeness 141

eight Courage 155

nine Community 177

Acknowledgments 197

Notes 199

Foreword

In my years of singleness, it felt like there was an invisible standard we were all trying to reach: *faithful singleness*. None of us knew exactly what faithful singleness was; we just knew it was chaste and pure; it was servant-hearted and communal; it was cheerfully available for our married friend's needs; it was always available for behind-the-scenes church functions; it was putting yourself out there, but not *too out there*; it was displaying the fruit of the Spirit at home, but with a new set of strangers with every new lease.

Here's what I know about those years of singleness: they were *exhausting*.

I'm not saying there aren't years of exhaustion in marriage too: there are. But there was a kind of exhaustion in singleness that was born from going at it alone for years on end. At the end of the day, the bills were mine alone, the budget was mine alone, and the bed was mine alone. My rubric for what faithfulness was in theory was almost always just tested by me and me alone. Faithfulness to this day, these finances, this bill, this housemate, this home, this car (and its maintenance), and more. And *everything*. My fidelity was to God, yes, but on earth, my fidelity was pledged to no one person forever.

The church might teach about covenant relationships and friendships, but most of the time these lessons are taught by those who are married, who have a construct for earthly covenant that informs how they understand it broadly. An unmarried person understands covenant in entirely different ways. It took me a long time to learn that the way I understand covenant was not lesser, but in some ways better. That in my *faithful singleness*, I had something to offer those trying to be faithfully married. That at the end of the day, our faithfulness isn't to our individual attachments but wholly to God, and therefore truly faithful singleness looks very much the same as faithful marriage: It means being chaste and pure, servant-hearted and communal, attentive to the needs of others, having courage in relationships, producing the fruit of the Spirit in our home with *whoever* we live with: roommates, spouses, children, or parents.

Melissa Zaldivar gets this. Every person who knows Melissa has seen her wrestling with these elements during her years as an unmarried person. Melissa has been a faithful single because she is a faithful *person*. She shows up for her community, she prays for her friends, she helps where there is need, she is patient with the old and the young, she is kind without discrimination, and so much more. She is an example to me still, now as a married person, of what faithfulness to Jesus looks like in a community. I honestly cannot think of very many people I'd trust to write this book (a book I wish had existed in my years of singleness!), and I am very happy to offer the foreword on it.

Get Over Here is a book about what it means to be a Christ-following *human*, written by an unmarried person with a unique vantage point (a vantage point that the church very much needs to hear more from). It is a book about how to love one another instead of othering those who are in different seasons of life. Melissa offers practical advice for those who are unmarried in the church, but also counsel for the ones who love the unmarried ones in their church. More than that, though, she offers that universal cry of "Me too!" for the ones who are still sleeping alone in beds they never imagined for themselves at this age or stage in their life.

You will find a care-filled and careful companion in Melissa, a truly faithful person. My prayer is that as you finish this book, you have hope that you can be this kind of person and find these kinds of people in your life too.

Lore Ferguson Wilbert, author

Introduction

the state of the union

There are countless ways that I sense my singleness, but none are a spectacle quite like showing up to a wedding reception and hearing the distinctive and percussive intro to "Single Ladies (Put a Ring on It)" by Beyoncé. The DJ shouts for all the eligible bachelorettes to come to the dance floor. The crowd, mostly couples, turns for a moment to watch the festivities like it's the freaking Hunger Games. All of the actual single ladies reluctantly gather and stand together in a clump, waiting for the bouquet toss.

Or we don't. For some of us, we step aside. Perhaps we're too weary from years of doing this literal song and dance because the only moment single people are truly acknowledged at a wedding is in this strange instance of people wondering, "Who is going to get married next?"

I know I'm not the only one tired of this ritual. It's the perfect moment to take a bathroom break, right?

I swear, if I ever get married, I'm going to play "Single Ladies" and then hand all the singles Target gift cards and thank them for their service. The idea that single people provide our entertainment is one of the more *Gladiator*-esque things that is wrong with how we approach single-ness. And the longer I've walked out of my apartment into the wide, wild world without a ring on my finger, the more I have been bombarded by the fact that maybe we've been approaching singleness and how it influences us in the wrong way altogether.

The way we approach a conversation deeply matters, es-pecially when we're stepping into territory that can be tender around the edges and all the way through to the middle. And sometimes when people aren't approaching topics or experiences that are familiar to them, they can launch right in without giving their tone or delivery a second thought.

Most conversations can be started casually, and there's not much concern about potential hiccups or shortsighted-ness. For example, we love to lead with topics like sports or current events or weather. We're all cheering for the same teams or watching the same shows or being influenced by the same atmospheric pressure. It's an easy way to con-nect with people who are new to us. But as we get to know others more, we can get more specific: Tell me about your job! Tell me about your family! Tell me what you're doing this summer! These common points of conversation are not problematic in and of themselves. But what do we do when someone doesn't have a family of their own beyond their family of origin? Or what if they don't have a spouse or a partner to talk about?

Never mind the fact that when friends attempt to check in with our lived experience, it can feel like they're working through a checklist. And once the usual topics of work or other updates end, the conversation stalls a bit. Then, once we're cornered one-on-one and they want to have a deeper conversation, the topic turns (inevitably) to our love lives.

Meet anyone recently?

How are things on the romance front?

What do you think about [insert potential suitor's name here]?

The challenge is this: the conversation is not centered around what we have, but what we do not have.

When someone has a child and you ask about their child, it's straightforward. Or when they have a job and you ask about their job, it's understandable. But when someone is childfree and you ask them when they're going to have a kid, it sucks the air right out of their lungs. When someone is job searching and you tell them that there are so many great jobs, it can undercut the endless hours they've spent sending résumés only to never get so much as a rejection email.

There is a big difference between asking about what someone has and leading with what they don't have. Inquiring about singleness is not like asking about the weather, right? It's opening someone's mail and reading it in public, and it does more damage than the asker may intend.

Besides the intensely personal nature of asking about our relationship status when we're often wanting it to be different, we also live in a culture that sees singleness as a problem to solve.

So it's no wonder we put on an extra layer of protection before going for coffee with a friend in case they start asking us about our dating life. We head into family dinners bracing for our aunties or grandparents to start suggesting they're ready to see us get hitched and have some kids. We're in a constant state of preparedness—like stepping onto a minefield, each step moving us forward with care and a bit of hesitation. Sometimes, we make it through the field without a scratch. Other times, we are left to nurse our own wounds after comments are made or looks are given. But no matter the outcome, we are worn out from the constant energy that needs to be stored up in our bodies and hearts so it can be spent navigating this world and these relationships.

I know the cringe that creeps up when someone addresses singleness from the pulpit after talking about their smokin' hot wife. I know the feeling of not belonging or wondering if people feel sorry for me because I don't have a date to an event or if they're going to ask if the friend I brought is someone I'm actually dating. I have been in that place where I've wondered what my future would look like, how I'm going to afford to buy a house, and if I did, would I only be filling it with my things? Photos of only my family on the fridge. Only my favorite foods in the pantry. Only my records beside my record player.

The apartment I currently live in in Massachusetts is lovely and feels like home in some ways, but every piece of decor or photo in a frame is my own. Hand-drawn artwork on display is from children at church or my nieces and nephews. Books on the shelves are about New England history or my own interests, and the pages have been turned and marked and worn over the course of my life.

I don't have my husband's toothbrush sitting in the toothbrush holder, nor his razor in the medicine cabinet. His shirts don't hang in the closet next to my sweaters. His keys aren't sitting in the tray with mine.

Because I am not married.

I do not share my life in the most intimate ways with anyone else. Even in the seasons I have had roommates, we had our own spaces. I'd never put a poster on my roommate's wall, and she'd never put her favorite seltzer on my shelf. We would live together, but we were still single. Over the years, I learned to make a life for myself that didn't include a partner. And over the years, I started to make peace with my relationship status, but with each major life transition and subsequent move, I knew in many ways that I'd have to start again with friendship and building community, and it felt so daunting to know that I would live in a new city without being able to have familiar faces to turn to for a little while.

I had already moved a few times in my twenties, and each transition from one place to the next changed me in some way because it pulled me from the people I loved. But each new city also brought opportunities and unique experiences. Austin had amazing culture and food. Fayetteville came with college town charm. I lived in Nashville for three years, more or less, and it was a hub of evangelical culture in America, right in the middle of the Bible Belt. There is no shortage of churches or para-church organizations or biblically-punny coffee shops or Chick-Fil-As in those parts. I enjoyed my time there and was challenged by the community of creative, Jesus-loving people, but something in me kept longing to go *back* for the first time to a place I loved.

I remember making a list in my head of reasons to move my life to Massachusetts and reasons to stay rooted in Tennessee. On the one hand, I *loved* New England. Since I'd gone to grad school there, I knew I would be going back to a great community of kindreds (albeit most of them married), and I would be able to settle in a place that felt like home. I loved the candles in the windows in winter and the slow picnics by the sea in summer. On the other hand, I would be more likely to find a potential partner in the South just because Christian faith was much more common. Churches abounded and a younger demographic meant increased chances of finding a like-minded match.

Better odds, sure, but it felt odd to use that as motivation to stay.

As I prayed over this decision, something in me knew to say goodbye to the South and that New England was where I needed to be for this next season of life. So I rented a U-Haul, asked my friend Ivanna to join me for a few days on the road, and headed north. In retrospect, it's wild that someone let us rent a giant truck, fill it up ourselves, attach my actual car to the back of it on a trailer, and drive from Tennessee to Massachusetts.

As a woman who has to go it alone, I don't know what I would have done if Ivanna wasn't there.

Well, actually, I do: I would have done it by myself.

Much of the single experience is this by-ourselves-ness, right? And it's not that we don't have friends. We're not truly alone in life, but we are facing each struggle and milestone by ourselves.

How will I make this month's mortgage or rent payment?

Where can I fit in the things I love to do with the things that I have to do?

What's the best time to take a vacation this year?

What happens if I get sick or have to miss that party or the fridge dies or my flight comes in later than the shuttle runs?

Other people may have a partner to process these questions with, but that's a luxury we just can't afford. It isn't an option for us to turn to a partner and say, "What do you think?" Our circumstances may seem similar, but the way we experience those circumstances is wildly different.

It's not that our troubles are more significant or our experiences more profound; we're just facing them without the warmth of another person standing shoulder to shoulder with us, walking hand in hand into the unknown.

No, we take each step forward by ourselves.

. . . .

I'd never seen my new Massachusetts apartment in person before leaving Nashville. My friend Julie had gone to visit it for me. And my friends Tim and Ann arrived early on moving day, looked for issues, and made sure the keys worked. They did a quick sweep and determined there was a little stain on the carpet so they got a can of carpet cleaner from the local hardware store and treated it. The leftover cleaner is still under the sink, five years later.

When we pulled up, a few hours later than expected, we were met by other church friends I had made when I first lived in Massachusetts while in school. It had been four years since I'd left that little Baptist church, but these friends had stayed in touch when I'd left to go on new adventures, and I had occasionally visited them. Still, they had no obligation to show up when I returned. We were friends, yes, but it had been a while.

I had been fully ready to arrive and move all the items in the truck with Ivanna. But, as it turns out, they hadn't forgotten me.

As we arrived, my friend Clay waved us into our parking spot, and he opened the back. I stumbled out of the driver's seat, and he gave me a joyful hug and said, "Tell us where things go—you're not going to move anything big." He eagerly put on his work gloves, and I looked up to see a few other familiar faces greeting me as other friends walked down the stairs of the porch. Clay's wife, Laura, was there and had brought drinks to share. Next, I saw my pastor, Bobby, and his wife, Julie, and then I saw Tim and Ann and my friend Sarah.

In what felt like less than an hour, these heroes had literally done all the heavy lifting and my apartment was full of boxes and there was an exhale of finally arriving. The apartment was everything I had prayed for, which was only two things: well-lit and well-insulated (a true win for the northeastern winter). It had two little rooms upstairs that I could use as an office and a guest room (as long as you aren't too tall, because the ceilings are slanted. It's fine).

I had a setup for a twin-sized bed and a queen. When they were unloading the queen-sized bed, the assumption was that it would go in my room downstairs, but I told them, "No. It goes in the guest room."

My room gets the twin bed.

I had made this arrangement for years in other places before, but now these friends were bearing witness to it. My reasoning for it is practical because the truth is this: The majority of my friends are married, so when they stay in the guest room, they're probably bringing a spouse. So it makes sense that they get the bigger bed in that space. I understand that everyone has their preferences, but I've just never liked sleeping in a big bed.

Rolling over in the morning and reaching out into a sea of sheets with no one in them had worn on me over the years, so at some point, I decided to have a twin bed to only take the space of one person. It wasn't about taking up less space or not deserving more, but about me embracing the reality of being solo. I had to face it head-on and wrestle through some big feelings. I've found that Jesus carries my emotions a whole lot more compassionately than I give Him credit for, so when it feels uncomfortable or emotionally hard to be in a twin bed, we can talk it out.

This is what I'm learning about Jesus: I get to be vulnerable in front of Him and tell Him exactly how I am feeling, and it's never too much for Him. The beauty of His infinite nature means He endlessly carries our heartache and our wholehearted joy.

As my friends heaved the queen mattress upstairs to the guest room, I found myself right between those emotions. Many struggles in my singleness have been subtle and barely obvious to my married friends. There's always something beneath each achievement or new life stage—moving is never just moving. Even if you're surrounded by people you love who are graciously helping you settle in, you still feel that sting of reality when they all go home and you're left on your own, assembling an IKEA shelf with an unpronounceable name.

There are a thousand little tasks and choices that we single people have to process through, and it becomes second nature after a while. When we grocery shop, we think strategically because foods are often portioned for families. When we drop off the car at the mechanic, we have to figure out a ride ahead of time to get back home. When we get sick, we have to rally to go get supplies before crawling into bed because once we're down, we're down for the count, and usually people aren't texting to see how we feel.

Sometimes, when I bring up these exact struggles with married friends, I just want them to understand my experience, but I find that almost immediately I am met with a barrage of solutions. Well-meaning friends have done this for ages. And I get that they're trying to help, but respectfully? I have already considered the fact that I can buy a big portion of ground beef and then *freeze* it. Or buy a whole pack of hot dogs and then *freeze* them. Or buy a full loaf of bread and then *freeze* it.

The problem isn't the fact that I don't know how to preserve hot dogs; it's that they are sold in an eight-pack that will go bad a few days after it opens. And even more so, I can't stomach the reality that as a person living alone, I am expected to just eat frozen food all the time.

As a native Californian, I am used to phrases like "Always fresh, never frozen"—a boast of the burger chain In-N-Out that proclaims the importance of fresh food. So, frozen as the default? No thank you. Further, by offering these obvious solutions, it feels like my non-single friends are just ignoring the real tension felt in the moment: I am one person, and this package of food is meant for several.

When I share my singleness experience, let me tell you what I'm not looking for: pro tips on how to get the most bang for my buck. I'm not eager to hear feedback on how to be more efficient with my overwhelm. I know about freezers and fractions, but I'm tired of doing the math to halve recipes and plan meals knowing that I'm going to eat leftovers

time and time again just to get through the smallest pack-
ages of perishable goods. So most of the time, I just end up
not buying the food I really want because the portions don't
make sense and I'm too emotionally exhausted to make it
work. It is very un-fun to plan out twenty-one meals this way
(most of which will be eaten alone, thankyouverymuch).

Here's the thing. I don't want troubleshooting; I want
tenderness.

I'm processing and lamenting and trying to make sense
of living life single, further isolating myself in the process. I
forget the toll that topics like marriage or love or dating can
take on me, like walking to the sandbar as the tide is rising,
not considering the subtle undertow that is pulling me out
to sea, away from the steadiness of the shore.

I start to feel overwhelmed and try my best to get back
to safety, but there are moments when the water is too high
and I'm caught in a current and desperately need a lifeboat,
when a beacon shines on the horizon and potential comfort
approaches, but instead I'm met with, "Have you tried putting yourself out there?"

No, Martha. I haven't considered that what I really need
on top of all of my own overwhelm is to rally the energy to
put on makeup and find someone who isn't catfishing on
the internet and answer questions about my favorite color
until they ask me to coffee only to reveal that they "consider
themselves spiritual" and don't go to church.

Talk about a sinking feeling.

Perhaps one of the trickier parts of being single is being in
community with those who aren't. It's not like my married
friends set out to misunderstand or offend. And it's not as
though I'm being cryptic in an attempt to be mysterious or

misunderstood. I certainly do not hate my partnered friends, nor do they see me in an overwhelmingly negative light. It's just too easy to forget that we're standing on common ground more than we realize when it feels like our relationship status is supposed to be the most important thing about us.

And when we forget to look down at said common ground, we lose touch. We leave one another behind. And our once-close friendships from childhood or college or our twenties are suddenly divided as everyone pairs off. We don't know we're just missing them until it comes out sideways as judgment or cynicism.

So, we step back.

Stop checking in.

And call it "growing apart."

Surely this sort of casual coexisting isn't what Scripture means when it tells us we actually belong with one another. Surely the call to bear one another's burdens was meant to be lived out.

There's a well-known passage in the Bible that says this: "Rather, speaking the truth in love, we are to grow up in every way into him who is the head, into Christ, from whom the whole body, joined and held together by every joint with which it is equipped, when each part is working properly, makes the body grow so that it builds itself up in love" (Eph. 4:15–16 ESV).

This seems like an obvious statement: a body works together because each part matters and does its job. We need hands to hold and eyes to see and ears to listen and legs to walk. This feels straightforward enough. What has caught my attention in this passage time and time again is the phrase, "when each part is working properly."

26

This means that you can't just have a foot—it needs to work properly. You can't just have eyes—they need to work properly. You can't just have a leg—it needs to work properly. If these parts don't work the way they're supposed to, the whole body is affected.

I once had surgery on my wrist because a cyst was resting on my nerve, causing all kinds of other issues. It was tender at any sudden jolt, which meant that when a dog jumped up to greet me or I needed to hold a baby for more than a minute or I was writing for long stretches, pain would get in the way.

It wasn't too major an operation. A few hours of surgery, and I came out with four small incisions and a cast. The cast hindered my mobility and limited my grip, but I adapted.

At first, I just did things with my left hand, assuming I wasn't going to have any other problems if I just avoided using my right arm. But a few days after surgery, I found that my back was hurting and my shoulders were tired, and I understood that I was compensating for what my wrist couldn't properly do. It was taking a toll on my entire body.

Two and a half weeks later, I got my cast off. I was so sure this would make things much simpler because my right hand—the dominant one—was finally back in action. When the nurse removed all the pieces of my cast, my arm went limp. It was wobbly and seemed to be made from the same stuff as Gumby. Surprised, I tried to pick up my arm, but it was behaving as if there was no sensation, and then suddenly I felt incredible pain. I couldn't control my hand well and slight movements made me yelp because the wrist just wasn't ready to get back to work. I couldn't even turn a doorknob. Here I thought I'd just skip right out the door, but this was going to take time.

Months later, I sat at a dinner with my friend Simi who is a physical therapist, and she casually said, "You know why your wrist felt like that? Because it only takes three days to atrophy. Two weeks doesn't seem like a long time, but it really does a number on your muscles."

A few hours of surgery.

A few weeks in a cast.

Recovery that took over six months.

When a part of the body isn't working properly, all of the body is affected. I was doing the proper routines and exercises, but the healing process was arduous and annoyingly lengthy.

My wrist was supported in the best possible position, but imagine if something went wrong at the start of the healing process.

For example, I was only dealing with muscle, but when a bone breaks, there's a new layer to the healing process because it has to be properly aligned and set so the limb can work again. If it isn't set just right, you could be faced with something called a malunion. This, as the name suggests, is a bad union. Something is out of alignment and there will be consequences.

According to Boston Children's Hospital, "As a result [of malunion], the limb may be bent, twisted, or both. Depending on which bone is involved and how severely the bone is out of alignment, a malunion can impair function and mobility in the affected limb."[1]

At times, you can get away with a super slight malunion. It's not ideal, but it's survivable. On the other hand, if it needs attention and doesn't get it? You stop functioning the way you're meant to.

The Greek word in Ephesians 4:15–16 for "properly working" insinuates supernatural work that is productive. As in, not just a casual, do-your-job work, but a you-were-meant-to-do-this-job work. As believers, we are like a body that is meant to do something that doesn't rely only on ourselves. We are called to work properly toward a purpose that God Himself is inviting us to partake in.

So many of our relationships and so much of our trust between married and single people have been lost because of breaks that aren't healing right. I wonder if we're left with malunion instead of union. On the outside, all seems well, but internally something is amiss.

I know that I have a myopic view and a history that is just mine, but I also know my overall experience isn't unique either.

It doesn't take much during a gathering of single people to start listing the heartache we carry as a result of our relationship status. We exchange dating horror stories, feelings of exhaustion, and bouts of wondering if we'll always be alone. One friend was told that he wouldn't be hired on staff at a church unless he had a wife. Yet another lamented feeling restless every holiday when she's alone with no plans. People don't often think of inviting single people to Easter dinners or Memorial Day cookouts.

Or perhaps it makes me think of countless stories of those who are told that if they play their cards right, they will find The One.

Being single becomes a liturgy of sorts with movements and worn-in words that guide us through well-meaning (or sometimes not so well-meaning) conversations. You learn when to sit and when to stand and what phrases are repeated weekly:

"No, I haven't met any cute guys lately."

"Yes, I am 'putting myself out there.'"

"Yes, he was wonderful, and we did break up."

"No, no. Don't feel bad about it. It happens."

We're out here repeating the same things and hearing the same things and experiencing the same things, and honestly? I am ready for us to have new conversations. I'm ready for us not only to feel like we belong at the table but to live into the truth that we get to host.

What if we were known for hosting parties, not just longing for a plus-one? Our God has given us this life, and it is wild and it is intense and it sometimes feels like pulling our hair into a ponytail and rolling up our sleeves. It takes a bit of grit and can sometimes leave us a bit sore, but I promise you: There is goodness on the other side.

I wish that someone had told me when I was in college or even earlier that life can be beautiful and fulfilling even if I don't have a partner. I wish someone had normalized singleness in a way that was compelling and courageous. I wish I had known that I wasn't less of a Christian or missing out on God's best for me just because I didn't have a husband.

In fact, we are invited to fully pursue the good things in life. Full stop.

No matter how you are coming into this book, I want you to know that your needs aren't any less important just because you're single. In fact, they're the same as everyone else's and need to be fulfilled just like everyone else's. These are God-given needs: You were made for companionship and commiseration and connection and commitment. You were made to know communication and consistency and closeness and courage and community. Each of these topics needs to be discussed, because we've been shoving some or all of them to the side, assuming we aren't meant to feel certain ways or we're waiting for our relationship status to change before we can live fully into them.

You can live a connected, committed, and courageous life now.

You can experience commiseration, closeness, and community now.

You can know companionship, consistency, and good communication now.

This book is about how to do. It's about how to be. How to move toward. How to bear witness. How to carry. How to celebrate. How to walk into a room and know that you belong, not despite your singleness, but because of it.

Also? This book is about making sure that we don't fall through the cracks and that our fellow single brothers and sisters don't fall through the cracks either. I often wonder what would happen if we paused and noticed those who have one foot out the door and said, "Wait, come back. You belong here with everyone else. Get over here, friend."

We were made for working together within holy community, but all the tensions and breaks between single and married people have left all of us unable to turn the doorknob and open up with one another. It's too painful. The muscles are atrophied. The bones aren't set right.

For every crack that has led to malunion, for every invitation that was not extended, for every moment of not being sure if you're allowed to long for good things, know that you are here on purpose and Jesus has not just forgotten about you. He didn't set you aside; He set you apart.

No mistake was made, no blessing was withheld because of something you did or did not do. And we're not hopelessly broken, forever stuck in a state of malunion with the world around us. We're just not always aligned, and it's taking its toll.

There is one way to heal a malunion—and I think you know exactly what it is. It involves getting uncomfortable and breaking. It's time to break up with the crooked ways we're approaching our singleness, our friendships, our churches, our *lives*. It may feel awkward and will likely be painful at times and take some work, but I do believe that we can make a full recovery.

My hope for these pages is that each of us can take stock of what's going on in our heads and our hearts and readjust our position in a way that allows us to work alongside others properly, regardless of relationship status. To, out of a heart for healing, ask big questions and allow ourselves to be cared for in practical and necessary ways. To be realistic about our own limited perspective and capacity and get very gentle. You cannot expect that heavy lifts and heavy hearts are so easily mended.

Do not read this book in a hurry. Read it like a guide that takes you one step at a time to a worthwhile place. Slow your roll. Take each step with intention. Consider these chapters as an opportunity to pay attention to the pain and places of misaligned values you have carried for all these years.

You were made to be here, exactly this single, and it is good that you are at the party. Your singleness is not a curse. It does not label you as unlovable—and it most certainly does not disqualify you from community. In fact? It might just equip you to invest fully right where you're at. Because you were made to be part of God's family—right down to your bones.

one

Companionship

When I was living in Nashville, I moved into a whole house by myself and lived alone for the first time. I moved in next door to my friend Sandra, who had floated the idea past me when her neighbors moved out suddenly. My other friends were all settled into their leases so none of them were available to join me, and I decided that if I was going to be alone, I was going to have to face it sooner or later.

The neighborhood was full of young families, and there was probably a bit of mystery around this young single woman who lived by herself and covered the walls with sticky notes because she was working on her first book manuscript. I'm sure my neighbors thought that I was unusual because I introduced myself to all of them in the first week. No time was wasted. I wanted to be friendly, yes, but also? If we're being honest? I wanted to know who was around in case something happened.

I was paying my own rent and my own utilities and my own internet bill by myself. I was trying to make the most of the IKEA furniture I had bought or found, trying to fill an empty home with whatever could take up space.

One night, Sandra and I sat at her kitchen counter, and I expressed to her how strange it felt to live alone when I had spent all my life until that point living with other people. "I love your twenties because it's like you're puppies, living all on top of each other," Sandra reminisced. I had been a metaphorical puppy for much of my life up to that point. I first lived in a home with my family, and then I moved away to college in Chicago. There, I had a spectacular group of twenty-five or so women who became a sisterhood of sorts. We would get dressed up and walk around downtown Chicago for no reason except that we could. We would go out to dessert and ask to split the check, which in retrospect was probably really annoying to the server because there were so many of us. But we also were so poor that none of us could have footed the bill alone anyway.

Sometimes, we would sneak onto the roofs of local hotels and take photos and upload them into albums on a new website called Facebook. Other times, we would come back to campus, invigorated by the frigid tundra of Chicago, and warm up by having dance parties in the lounge that connected all of our rooms. We were in that fun space between teenager and adult where you got to figure out how to live on your own but you never were by yourself.

After college, when I moved to Massachusetts the first time, I lived in an old estate house that rose up in the center of campus, and there were eighteen or so other women who shared the space. It was a large brick building, so even though we were together, there was a bit more independence. As I made friends on campus, mostly with the student wives, we would meet every week for what we called Drink Night. The irony, of course, was that it was a dry campus. Nevertheless, we called it Drink Night because I think it made us feel a little bit wild. The location varied, but after the kids went to bed, we would sit around and laugh and regale each other with stories about that week's mishaps and adventures in parenting, marriage, and my dating life (as I was the only single person there).

A few years later, right after my graduation from seminary, I lived in a big brick house in Austin, Texas, with fellow interns. Then, I moved to Nashville and signed a lease with some women I had never met who were friends of a friend. In retrospect, I am so glad I wasn't murdered then and there and that they turned out to be wonderful humans.

Each place I'd lived up to that point was unique and offered a community that was built-in. In that sweet home in Nashville, I learned how to be single in a whole new way.

Prior to that moment, I'd been surrounded by housemates or roommates. Everyone was in everyone else's business. But now? I could quietly go about my life and there wasn't someone to share meals with or debrief about the day. There wasn't anyone to check in. I was trying to learn about 401(k)s and planning for my future on my own, and when there was a loud sound in the middle of the night, it was up to me to investigate.

For all the adventure and joy of having my own place, being alone felt very, well, lonely. Living on your own is both wonderful and a bit sneaky-sad. I walked (and continue to walk) a tightrope between being glad to have my own space and longing for it to be filled.

I have lived by myself since that little house, and I have found that one of the most challenging parts of singleness is the fact that we have to make an effort if we want to experience companionship. We are not guaranteed to have someone around, and if we want intentional friendship, it's going to take some work.

Sure, I had my friend right next door, but it's different when you live in two different homes with two different life rhythms. She was a single mom and was regularly making space for youth sports and events and school while juggling a career in music and traveling on the weekends. I was a young professional with my first job that wasn't in ministry, and I suddenly had a bit more margin.

Some would say she and I were in different life stages or different seasons, but those terms are some of the most unfair we can offer when we talk about singleness. In fact, we need to pause and think about the language we use to describe this very topic.

More often than not, when someone is trying to explain how someone who is married has different priorities or at least a different experience than someone who is single, they say that the two individuals are in different "life seasons." Or perhaps they will say that they are in different "life stages." This is common language that is widely accepted, and I am sure you have heard someone refer to your "life season" or "stage" of singleness as the status you fall under. But here's the thing: Language is important because it dictates the ethos of our lives.

To suggest that singleness is a "stage" insinuates that there are multiple stages that all build on top of one another and your goal is to get to the final stage. To suggest that singleness is a "season" insinuates that it is temporary, and you *will* move on from it. Both phrases indicate that singleness is not permanent. Using these terms actually robs us of an imagination for how full a life of singleness could be. And, whether people are aware of it or not, this way of thinking and wording makes us feel not only that we are behind but that we are infantile. Underdeveloped. Small.

If a single person never gets married, are they forever at stage one? Are they forever frozen in a season where it's always winter and never spring? Are they forced to face a fate of no diversity of experiences in the world around them?

Surely not.

Surely the Creator of the universe who Himself was never married does not see singleness as a cursed existence.

Paul was single and he called it good. Jesus never preached that marriage on this side of eternity should be our end goal. He never said that single people were missing out on kingdom work because of their relationship status. In fact, Paul makes the argument that single people are able to give themselves over to ministry in a unique and good and beautiful way *because* of their singleness.

Now I want to be clear: I am not suggesting that single people should be giving every waking moment to the work of God's kingdom and burn themselves out just because they do not have a partner. We often misinterpret that passage of Scripture as a mandate that single people must always be ready to jump in and say yes because they have endless free time.

To assume that single people have endless margin and free time is a very unfair assessment. As a result of being a single-income person living alone, all household responsibilities and logistics fall to me. I don't have someone to help carry the daily load. I may not be awake all hours of the night with a newborn, but that doesn't mean I am not lying awake at night stressed over other things. My alleged freedoms are often overtaken by the fact that there's not someone to help run errands or pay bills or do dishes or do other necessary tasks.

Yes, there are some flexible components to my life as a result of being unmarried. But there are some downsides as well. I think in general we need to stop keeping score, because all it's doing is making us a less united front as Christians, and we are not advocating for one another but rather assessing one another, which is no way to build true companionship.

Back to the language of stages and seasons.

How do we resolve this inadequate phraseology? How do we fairly talk about singleness and what it feels like? I would like to submit to you a simple word that I think could change our posture: *route*.

What if we are on the *route* of singleness? What if we are traveling to the same destination as everyone else but we are getting there a different way? The chief end of man and the calling we have as Christians are not different depending on our relationship status.

We are all headed to the same place. We are all moving toward Jesus. That said, the way we get there might look different.

As a single person, there will be different obstacles along the path that we travel. And married people will have a path they are traveling that also has its own obstacles. Metaphorically, we will see different things and weave in and out of different locations, but at the end of the journey, we all arrive on the same eternal shore.

Sometimes our paths overlap, and we see the same things and experience the same terrain, but other times, our ways look different—and that's okay! Each route is beautiful and terribly hard in its own way.

Using route language allows us to have compassion for one another and to see the value in each person's road. We are like hikers, and we all have days of fair weather and loveliness, but we also have days when clouds roll in and conditions get worse and we have to take cover. The route is lovely, but it is also incredibly exposing.

Having grown up in California, I have a deep appreciation for a good walk. The area I was raised in sits along the coastline, and rolling hills surround the town. When I make the cross-country flight to be with family, I reach out to the friends I've known my whole life, and more often than grabbing a meal, we take a walk.

Because walking is so dearly loved by my hometown, it's almost a joke that when I go home I average five to seven miles a day on foot. I'll walk with a friend for three miles at dawn and hear about her cats and the students she teaches, and then I'll walk two miles at lunchtime with another friend, who has a new baby and is trying to maintain sanity as she parents three littles. Then, as the sun is starting to set, I'll take yet another walk and hear how retirement is going for a beloved mentor.

There is something brilliant about walking and talking because it provides the perfect cadence for connection and companionship.

Some days, being single feels like going on walks with friends in short stints. We move along together at a similar pace and then go about our days. But other times? I wonder if singleness is like a long through-hike, where you hike several continuous long-distance trails, and it takes much more stamina than you may realize. It is not a quick one-mile walk or even a marathon that you train for, run, and then it's over. No, this is a day-to-day reality, and if you're going to walk it well, you have to prepare yourself for not only what you see coming but what you might not.

I once met a girl in college named Liesel who, along with her husband, Dave, became a long-distance hiker and has traversed her way across the United States several times. I love cardio, but I am not committed to making the wilderness my dwelling.

Liesel and Dave are what we call through-hikers, because they don't just hike a segment of a big trail like the Pacific Crest Trail or the Appalachian Trail—they start at the beginning, and they go all the way through.

This sort of journey is not for the faint of heart, and as I asked her about her experience of hiking in this way, her description could not be pulled apart from the experience of companionship. While hiking alone is certainly possible, it takes much more out of you mentally because there is no camaraderie.

She and Dave could not only tangibly help each other along the route but also be there to listen and process and offer insight. After having to cut another hike short due to weather earlier in the year, Liesel was panicking about an impending storm, and Dave gently reminded her that each hike would be different. When her brain wouldn't let her calm down on her own, his encouragement got her back to a sense of peace. He was able to enter into her anxiety with her and show her a way through it.

She told me, "We could be the person that the other needs when they aren't there yet."

Hearing their story reminds me that one of the most important things hikers need is companionship. And if singleness is like a through-hike? We're going to need companions. Whether it's meeting someone on the route and overlapping for a few miles or finding someone committed to the hike from start to finish, it allows for better morale and encouragement along the way. When you're hiking alone, it's easy to feel backed into a corner at times, and you need a companion to help process or prepare. The perspective that they bring can be absolutely vital.

My other friend Kristin once hiked five hundred miles through Spain one summer, and it changed some of her lifestyle. We used to just eat pizza and french fries when we wanted to hang out, but now we're trying to make healthier habits (though admittedly, this morning we planned our next pizza night while we walked). Sometimes it's dark out when we go for a walk, and in the cooler seasons, daylight is just breaking through the tree line as we get out of our cars. The sound of the gravel beneath our feet slowly wakes me up as we wander together along the trails of old farmland.

I thought that this habit of weekly walks would only wake me up or make me healthier, but I have been delighted to find that it has grounded me in profound ways and offered a chance for companionship that sets the tone for my whole day. This practice of rolling out of bed and into my running shoes, shuffling down the stairs to my car and turning on my windshield wipers to get rid of the dew is offering me a chance to be anchored.

As we walk, we talk about whatever is on our hearts or minds, and it gives us a start to our days that isn't just us alone in our own places. Starting my day with a conversation and connecting with a friend gives me a sense of companionship that carries me through long weeks where waking up and going to work early feels hard.

Kristin knows from that summer of through-hiking that there is something grounding about getting out and moving your feet, and she has passed that on to me too.

When Jesus begins His ministry, the first thing He does with His disciples is invite them in. He sees them in their places, and He invites them to join Him. He does not sit and wait, but actively moves and asks them to move with Him:

> As Jesus was walking beside the Sea of Galilee, he saw two brothers, Simon called Peter and his brother Andrew. They were casting a net into the lake, for they were fishermen. "Come, follow me," Jesus said, "and I will send you out to fish for people." At once they left their nets and followed him.
>
> Going on from there, he saw two other brothers, James son of Zebedee and his brother John. They were in a boat with their father Zebedee, preparing their nets. Jesus called them, and immediately they left the boat and their father and followed him. (Matt. 4:18–22)

Friendship takes an invitation, and companionship involves intentionality. These days, we try our best to manufacture depth, but only those two activating ingredients of invitation and intentionality can cause a reaction that allows us to build true companionship. Without both, we cannot make a plan for a long hike.

You'll notice that the author does not include a very long and drawn out back-and-forth in which Jesus tests the waters of who will be His disciples. No, He chooses a variety of disciples from different backgrounds and doesn't seem to be choosing the people who are the most desirable and popular. We spend so much of our lives trying to fit in with the popular crowd or idolizing individuals or having friend crushes when maybe we need to look around and see who is already along this section of our route. A lot of the time, the friendships that absolutely change our lives are found in the most unlikely yet ordinary places.

I met one of my college besties in the laundry room and another one when she walked into a mutual friend's dorm to rant about something and didn't know I was going to be there. Instead of offering to come back later, she just joined us, and the rest is history. Another close friend was found when I was passing through her town, and she and I decided to grab coffee on a whim. Yet another friendship was forged during long hours sitting in a marketing office trying not to lose our sanity or die of boredom. In fact, most of the women I know and cherish as dear friends were found when one of us simply invited and committed.

And now, we walk along our routes and encourage each other along. Companionship is not just about having things in common, but genuinely walking beside one another, fully present. The word *companion* comes from two Latin words that mean "to come" and "bread."

To gather and break bread.

To share a meal.

You have to be there—really be there. To make room and fill up your cup and put food on your plate, offering to do the same for someone else. To be a companion is to light a candle and share a table and engage in conversation, making eye contact and asking good questions. Long after the meal is over, you are still sitting there, telling stories of what was or what you hope will be. To enter someone's home and dine with them builds an intimate connection and, in our digital age, continues to be a rich point of community. You cannot share a meal with someone via the internet in the same way you do when you are in the same room.

That's not to say we cannot catch up with friends who are far away, but the root of our friendship is most often grown in shared moments.

It takes arranging schedules and planning travel and creating space. Companionship is a way of committing to one another, one meal (or moment) at a time. And as we build these relationships based on shared experiences, we find that the natural result is the ability to be vulnerable and at rest with one another. We stop putting our best foot forward and we start showing up right from work or in our pajamas or our workout clothes with our hair pulled back and our makeup removed. The clean and organized hiking gear becomes stained and tired and torn, but we keep walking together. We continue on, side by side, because it was never about how things appeared but the beauty of what has been revealed: genuine, season-after-season friendship.

One of my all-time favorite examples of this season-after-season friendship is from a book I collect called *The Wind in the Willows* by Kenneth Grahame. Written in the early 1900s, it's about animals who live in community and go on adventures. The primary character is a rather timid mole who decides one day to dig his way from his home underground to the surface; he discovers sunshine and grass and beauty and decides to venture forth, seeking what there is to see beyond the comforts he's used to. He meets a few fun characters, but the first and most dear is a water rat who acts as a sort of guide for him with his wild and enthusiastic spirit. The mole and the rat travel by boat and by car and by foot, and about halfway through the book, they are walking through the woods late at night to get back to town. The book begins with Mole leaving home, and now it has been months since Mole was there, and he honestly has forgotten about his previous life. Suddenly the scent of something familiar catches his nose.

He realizes they aren't far away from his long-abandoned home, and he calls out to Rat to turn around and join him. Unfortunately, Rat is too far up ahead to properly hear what Mole is clamoring about—the weather is getting tricky— and in his haste to make it to town before a snowstorm, Rat replies and tells Mole to just keep walking.

Mole desires companionship more than his home, so he complies and pushes aside his feelings of longing. After a while, when they are nearly back to town, Rat notices that Mole seems downtrodden, and, having no idea why, he starts asking him what's going on.

The scent of home is long gone, and Mole is lamenting that, as Grahame would say, "He had lost what he could hardly be said to have found."[1]

After a bit of investigating, Mole cracks open with a sobbing explanation:

The Rat, astonished and dismayed at the violence of Mole's paroxysm of grief, did not dare to speak for a while. At last he said, very quietly and sympathetically, "What is it, old

45

fellow? Whatever can be the matter? Tell us your trouble, and let me see what I can do."

Poor Mole found it difficult to get any words out between the upheavals of his chest that followed one upon another so quickly and held back speech and choked it as it came. "I know it's a—shabby, dingy little place," he sobbed forth at last brokenly: "not like—your cozy quarters—or Toad's beautiful hall—or Badger's great house—but it was my own little home—and I was fond of it—and I went away and forgot all about it—and then I smelt it suddenly—on the road, when I called and you wouldn't listen, Rat—and everything came back to me with a rush—and I wanted it!—O dear, O dear!—and when you wouldn't turn back, Ratty—and I had to leave it, though I was smelling it all the time—I thought my heart would break.—We might have just gone and had one look at it, Ratty—only one look—it was close by—but you wouldn't turn back, Ratty, you wouldn't turn back! O dear, O dear!"

Recollection brought fresh waves of sorrow, and sobs again took full charge of him, preventing further speech. The Rat stared straight in front of him, saying nothing, only patting Mole gently on the shoulder.

After a time he muttered gloomily, "I see it all now! What a pig I have been! A pig—that's me! Just a pig—a plain pig!" He waited till Mole's sobs became gradually less stormy and more rhythmical; he waited till at last sniffs were frequent and sobs only intermittent. Then he rose from his seat, and, remarking carelessly, "Well, now we'd really better be getting on, old chap!" set off up the road again over the toilsome way they had come.

"Wherever are you (hic) going to (hic), Ratty?" cried the tearful Mole, looking up in alarm.

"We're going to find that home of yours, old fellow," replied the Rat pleasantly; "so you had better come along, for it will take some finding, and we shall want your nose."[2]

Rat understood that home meant something to Mole and shifted his focus to the needs of his companion. He did not hesitate to provide what his friend emotionally needed. And he did not mind retracing their steps on a cold, snowy night, because friendship is not about convenience or timeliness. It isn't about keeping a schedule or a list or expectations. Rather, companionship in its truest form is about waiting and watching and listening and responding. We think about what's going on in the life of our companion, noticing their movements and attitudes and responses. The journey isn't just about the road we're traveling on but learning about the person we're traveling beside.

Some of us have been in friendships that were about reacting more than responding, or they may have been built on immaturity or shaky foundations. Perhaps you have rushed into a friendship and regretted that decision when a time of need arose. Maybe those experiences weren't so much about people having ill intent as much as people being ill-prepared for the terrain that the journey would require. And that's okay too! Not every friendship is forever.

Plenty of times, I have stepped into friendships I thought would last a lifetime only to find that they were seasonal. For a long time, I thought this was an indication of friendship failure, but I realized as I got older that the real indication was that each friendship served its purpose, and I could be thankful and still move on in peace and closure with that person.

I'm so thankful for the women on my dorm floor even though we don't regularly connect. I'm so joyful to have shared that big brick house with fellow seminarians, and I cheer them on from a distance as we all pursue what the

Lord has for us, but most of us don't keep in touch daily. With each new life movement, I have carried a handful of friendships with me, but many others changed when our circumstances changed. This is part of companionship as you grow up, and though it is painful at times, when we embrace the way our paths diverge, we can honor friendships for what they have been and have a sense of resolution.

Years ago, I taught a Bible study in the basement of my church, and because it was during the week at 10:00 a.m., the majority of women who attended were either retirees or stay-at-home moms. One woman, fantastically named Monie Fluth, attended every week. Monie lived much of her life overseas doing medical missions work with her husband. She had lost him fairly recently to a slow-moving condition and now she was active in a grief ministry. We became friends over the years, and I have been in awe of how Monie has chosen to just cherish everyone all the time. She sees friendship as an opportunity for companionship even if it's not for too much of the route.

One Sunday after the final song, our associate pastor got up and invited Monie to the front and announced that she was moving away to be closer to her daughter in the Midwest. I was absolutely shocked by this news because she had become such a dear part of our church community.

I invited her for dinner to try and soak her up as much as possible, and she told me all about how she will be living close to her daughter and how the church she will be attending is one that has supported her missions work so it already feels familiar. She said she would be living in a senior community within walking distance of the church itself.

She seemed so matter-of-fact and at peace about everything.

How could she be okay with this major life transition?
I thought.

And then I remembered: Monie has lived a lifetime of walking alongside others for a season, and this is just another opportunity to go walk alongside some new friends as she moves closer and closer to reuniting with her husband and being with Jesus. Monie is no longer afraid of friendships changing because she knows that the eternal weight of companionship outweighs saying goodbye.

One of the biggest lessons she's taught me is that a friend is a gift, and companionship is an opportunity, not a task.

We have a tendency to white-knuckle grip our friendships and assume that companions must be for a lifetime or they don't count. But when I look at my life as a route and my path as a hike, I see how God has given me multiple companions who have walked the terrain and warned me about conditions on the horizon. They have been caught by surprise alongside me or seen things coming that I didn't. Together, we have slid through the mud and gotten lost and stopped to take in stunning views.

Friendships are not here just to serve us or to make us feel better about ourselves or to give us some kind of identity that satisfies us down to our core. In fact, we see that Christ Himself is the truest companion who walks alongside us every single step of the way until we arrive at the end, which, it turns out, is total communion with Him. He not only gives us friends to walk alongside, but He is there as well, boots on and backpack full. He makes daily small talk and offers help when we are overwhelmed or overcome. He is a trail guide, familiar with every twist and turn, and the more that we experience Him in this capacity, the more we can learn to trust Him.

I am often afraid of what my route might entail.

What if writing makes me so vulnerable that I get hurt?

What if falling in love doesn't pan out and I travel more of this route by myself than I'd like?

What if I get lost and there isn't someone with me to help me slow my breathing and reassure me?

Rough conditions are forecasted, and I'm pacing around, vulnerable to things I cannot control. I look for the safety of a backup plan, worrying about what will happen if bad weather comes and the rain doesn't stop, and my matches get wet.

And then my anxiety is met by the nearness of Jesus, and it's as if He says, "What if your writing gives others a map so they can find their way back to the trail? What if you fall in love and it grows something beautiful in you? What if being alone allows you to rely on Me in ways that you otherwise wouldn't? What if you remember that I am always with you? What if I'm the one who carries waterproof matches?"

Right, right. We do not travel alone.

None of us know the terrain at the outset, but all of us discover it one day at a time, mile by mile. And as we learn the slope and pitch and texture of each new pathway, we have the opportunity to tell others what we wish we'd been told. I wish that someone had sat me down and said, "Listen. You're going to need better walking shoes on this route."

And this is the gift of the route, friend: We get to blaze a trail for others. With every coffee date or walk and talk, we get to give others hope that singleness is full of ups and downs and a whole lot of beauty. We get to tell the stories of our own missteps and mishaps, but we also get to give them the very good news that this route is one that offers incredible views and is well-traveled by so many incredible people who live full and beautiful lives.

Together, we get to rise up, tie our laces, and meet the day with joy, knowing that we are not alone, we have what we need, and our companions make the difference.

two

Commiseration

When I was eight years old, my parents gave me a camera. I gave no indication that I was interested in photography or documenting much of anything, but they had some hunch and decided to wrap one up and hand it to me. I eventually moved on to video and learned more about the art of film. The camera became the lens through which I saw the world, making silly short films with neighborhood friends and capturing behind-the-scenes stories of middle and high school.

The summer after my freshman year of college, I saved up to buy my first proper DSLR, and friends started asking me to capture photos of them. Sophomore year, two of my good friends got married and paid me two hundred dollars to be their wedding photographer. At the wedding, we laughed and they posed and we danced and it felt like something in me just came alive as I watched them go from engaged to married.

I was in Bible college and then enrolled in seminary, which meant there were lots of young loves, and I had the honor of documenting over forty weddings by the time I got my master's degree. I once traveled over twenty-five thousand miles in a year, and I wish I had understood how airline loyalty programs worked at the time.

Dozens of times, I have stood at the edge of a dance floor, camera lifted to my eye, finger on the shutter, waiting in anticipation for the next big move.

I have been there in that intimate space of a first look, watching a groom hold back tears as he sees his bride for the first time. I have clicked away as they embrace each other and whisper their vows and share a tender first kiss as husband and wife. I have watched them feed each other cake and take their first dance, his hand so carefully on her waist, her body slowly leaning into his.

And over the course of a wedding day, I watch them get closer and closer as they begin to settle into being husband and wife. They start to relax, their movements linger, and they go from being two to being one. I've witnessed it dozens of times and then I've gone home, joyful and exhausted.

It is a good and lovely thing to celebrate love and to make a life of the goodness of others finding it. But also? I have gone home to a quiet space and felt something deep in me feel unsettled. Like having a pebble in my shoe—I can keep walking, but not always comfortably. No, sometimes, I find myself walking with a limp along the route of singleness.

I remember one night in particular I had been capturing a wedding of dear friends out of town, and before I went to bed, I grabbed a few images for a sneak peek. I went to bed with images flashing through my mind of people jumping around on the dance floor as the groom wrapped his arms around his new bride, and she threw her arms all the way out like a little girl begging to be spun around over and over. But a few hours later, I woke up gasping and nearly in tears. I had recently walked through a breakup, and in my dream we were back together. He and I were sitting together on a boat floating along the shoreline of New England, and he was looking at me like he'd found something special. Clearly confused as to how we were suddenly dating again (and also crushing it on the pun front), I asked him, "Haven't we been in this same boat before?" He smiled and nodded and told me he wanted to marry me. I felt held.

But then I woke up. And when I did, I was flooded with the heavy ache of realizing that it was dark and I was alone, and we were very much so not together. I sat up and wiped the tears off my cheeks and felt as though this wound had been torn open and my heart was bleeding out and I would never be okay again. I was shaky for days with this image of us together that only lived in my imagination.

I wish I could tell you that the joyful moments are all that there are. I wish that you could go to a wedding and never again think about the fact that you're not married. I deeply want there to be a scenario where we never feel the longing or unmet desire that comes from waking up in the middle of the night alone.

I am in my midthirties and still feel restless and lonely in moments of vulnerable singleness. And I do not like the way that I question my value on days when I wake up a bit more insecure. I do not like that I'm so critical of my own sadness over singleness. I do not like that I lose compassion for myself.

There are times we see the ache coming, but sometimes it comes out of nowhere, sticking to us like sap that we cannot get off without scrubbing until we're raw. It's not the anniversary of something hard, nor is there anything in particular that triggers the feeling that overcomes me when I open my eyes, but it feels like aimless wandering, even when I'm at home. Suddenly, I am in unfamiliar territory even though I've lived in the same apartment for five years.

It is a delicate dance, being single into your thirties and beyond. People stop telling you that you have plenty of time. They stop telling you "You're next" at a wedding. They stop asking about dating with excited tones and instead ask with a thin layer of pity.

Sometimes, the ache doesn't stick around for too long, and brushing my teeth and washing my face and drinking extra water and eating a good meal helps a tremendous amount. Other times, it takes a bit more intentionality, and I need to go on a walk or linger a bit longer with my Bible and journal. But if I'm honest? Sometimes pulling out my Bible and journal makes it more achy. It's as if I'm pulling out a first aid kit because I know that I'm bleeding, and I'm acknowledging that my wound is too deep to ignore.

It's one thing to turn to Jesus because of abundance and love and warm fuzzy feelings, but it is another thing to turn to Him when you *know* He's your only and last hope. There is a feeling of fear that enters the room because I worry that He might not be enough, and then we've used our last bandage only to bleed through it.

And I start to wonder: What if He's not coming to rescue me, and I'm left alone in these trenches?

We worry that Jesus isn't coming back for us—we're afraid that we might be met by His desire to stay away from our wounds, not get closer to them.

I am often surprised to find that the Jesus I make up in moments of panic is not the Jesus I encounter. The Jesus I encounter sits gently beside me and looks at my wound and says, "I've seen this before and it's going to be okay."

Because commiseration is the ability to sit down and have empathy. And empathy is looking someone in the eye and saying, "Oh, friend. I have been there, and I am so sorry."

Because this isn't what we signed up for, you know? We didn't plan on some of these plot twists. I didn't dream of marriage as a little girl, but I also felt a certain amount of concern for my friend Hannah who got married as an old maid of *twenty-seven years old*. We still laugh about it to this day now that I'm eight years older than she was, and I have no ring on my finger.

Our hearts are complex landscapes of genuine happiness for others who find romantic love mixed with a fear that maybe all we'll ever be is happy for someone else. We hold celebration in our hands as everyone floods the dance floor, but during a water break, when the summer breeze calls us to step away from the chaos, there's that moment, right? The one where we stand on the outskirts of the party and feel, even if just for a moment, that we're alone.

So let me say this: Oh, friend. I have been there, and I am so sorry.

I'm sorry that this isn't what you thought would be your story. I'm sorry that you've walked through a breakup and each morning you wake up, reminding yourself that you're no longer with them. I'm sorry that you've never been kissed or held or told "I love you" by someone you thought could be your forever. I'm sorry for the comments and the assumptions and the implications made that have left you feeling a sense of lament.

Because that's the word for what we're carrying.

Lament.

How do we hold space for the grief of singleness while still making room for meaning and hope and joy and even celebration?

I think it starts by slowing down enough to know what we're feeling. To give our feelings names like *anger* and *sadness* and *anxiety* and *disappointment*. If we don't use language for our current state, it will be nearly impossible to find a way toward being anchored again. We have to call this what it is before we can call out to others.

Because here's the thing: One of the only ways we get out of the pit is by calling out to others.

I have friends—some married, some not—who I reach out to for different reasons, but I have found that having a handful of people you can truly commiserate with is a game changer. I have friends who I can call and say, "Hey, can I just tell you something that's hard?" and they'll listen and not try to fix things. We carefully skirt the line between processing and venting and ask Jesus for wisdom in how to approach our pain points.

Look for someone you admire who doesn't complain just to hear the sound of their own voice but is looking to live out wisdom in daily life. Find a friend who pursues Jesus as the ultimate Comforter and sits with you in the dark and allows you to feel the weight of these complex emotions without trying to make them just go away. A friend who listens is like the rarest of finds at your local antique store. That sort of connection is timeless and surprising and delightful, and it feels a bit like God is winking at you because it works out so poetically. I understand that this type of friendship doesn't happen often, and it is my prayer that you will one day know, if you don't already, what it means to have someone in your life who you can text when your head is hanging low and your shoulders are curled inward.

To commiserate is sometimes to just bear witness to someone's story. And to do that in a healthy way, we need to make sure our hearts are being aligned toward Christ. We aren't just out here allowing the bitterness of a moment to ruin every meal. No, we're fighting to sit with one another and then carry one another toward something good and healing and whole-making.

The word *shalom* is a well-known Hebrew term that loosely means "peace." But beyond that? It means "peace, prosperity, wholeness, completeness." This peace is given to us by God, and it has a way of anchoring us in the wildest of waters.

When we are losing our grip, Christ brings peace.

When we are sinking deep, Christ brings peace.

When we are not sure we'll ever recover from that heartache no one sees, Christ brings peace.

And one of the ways He does it most often is through the friends we have.

My friend Shelley and I started texting about a year ago when I was walking through something hard, and she would send me a heart emoji that just meant, "You are loved."

No explanation, no big inquiry. Just a simple heart to let me know that she was thinking about me as she raised her kids and cared for her community and made a life out in California. This simple gesture of sending a heart has carried me through times when I just needed to know someone saw me, someone was praying for me. When she walked through a tragedy of her own, the hearts took on even more meaning. Now they also meant, "Even in this mess, you are loved."

The weariness makes us feel like we have no safety net. If there is a medical emergency, there is no backup plan. If you get fired from your job, there is no additional funding from a joint account. If you get sick or injured, you have to figure out a way to be taken care of.

We don't want much, and yet somehow it feels like we're asking for too much. And when we lift our voices and say that we are unhappy or afraid or overwhelmed in any way, we are often met with encouragement that's not helpful. But what if the tables were turned? What if a new mom said she was exhausted, and I responded with, "Well, at least you have a child, what a blessing!"? Or perhaps more pointedly, what if someone who was struggling with infertility for a very long time was approached by a single person who asked, "So, are you pregnant yet?" every week when they saw each other at church?

That would be ridiculous! It would be so unkind! And yet, we are regularly sitting in the middle of those exchanges where people pick apart our personal lives and try to figure out what is wrong with us or what we need to improve in order to avoid the fate of being single, as if being single in and of itself is a death sentence.

So it's no wonder that discouragement bleeds into despair. It's no wonder the corners of our hearts get hard over time.

It's no wonder we're sometimes turning from commiseration to cynicism.

In John 11, we are told that Jesus is ministering to people when he receives terrible news of a friend's severe illness.

> Now a man named Lazarus was sick. He was from Bethany, the village of Mary and her sister Martha. (This Mary, whose brother Lazarus now lay sick, was the same one who poured perfume on the Lord and wiped his feet with her hair.) So the sisters sent word to Jesus, "Lord, the one you love is sick."
>
> When he heard this, Jesus said, "This sickness will not end in death. No, it is for God's glory so that God's Son may be glorified through it." Now Jesus loved Martha and her sister and Lazarus. So when he heard that Lazarus was sick, he stayed where he was two more days, and then he said to his disciples, "Let us go back to Judea." (vv. 1–7)

It says that Jesus loved Martha and Mary and Lazarus. These are not random acquaintances. No, they are beloved friends of Jesus. And when Lazarus is ill, Jesus decides to go to him.

But he's too late. Lazarus died before Jesus could get to him. When he finally makes his way to Judea, he is met by Martha.

> On his arrival, Jesus found that Lazarus had already been in the tomb for four days. Now Bethany was less than two miles from Jerusalem, and many Jews had come to Martha and Mary to comfort them in the loss of their brother. When Martha heard that Jesus was coming, she went out to meet him, but Mary stayed at home.

"Lord," Martha said to Jesus, "if you had been here, my brother would not have died. But I know that even now God will give you whatever you ask." (vv. 17–22)

Martha confronts Jesus with disbelief that He didn't show up for Lazarus. Mary doesn't even come out to meet Him. She's probably too lost in her grief, a mix of anger and sadness. Finally, she shows up:

When Mary reached the place where Jesus was and saw him, she fell at his feet and said, "Lord, if you had been here, my brother would not have died."

When Jesus saw her weeping, and the Jews who had come along with her also weeping, he was deeply moved in spirit and troubled. "Where have you laid him?" he asked.

"Come and see, Lord," they replied.

Jesus wept. (vv. 32–35)

Mary and Martha are both thinking the same thing: *If this had gone the way we'd hoped, if Jesus had shown up when we needed Him to, we would not be in mourning. We would be fine, and Lazarus would be alive.*

But instead of telling them that their grief is in vain and snapping His fingers and bringing Lazarus back from the dead right away, Jesus slows down, feels His own heartache, and weeps.

True commiseration meets us with compassion.

Jesus isn't here to teach a lesson or say, "Now, mourners: Stop it." No, He's here to be fully present with those who are in the rawest stages of grief, and although He will make all things right, He does not remove their sadness. He does not give them a list of silver linings. He does not give trite phrases to make them *feel better.*

No, He trades feeling better for feeling together.

This is the heart of our God.

Psalm 34:18 says it this way: "The LORD is close to the brokenhearted and saves those who are crushed in spirit." We serve a God who has been brokenhearted. There is nothing wrong with lamenting and being frustrated and upset that you are where you are and you have what you have—or that you do not have what you wish you had.

But it feels personal, right? As if when someone else gets married or engaged we're somehow falling further behind. We see announcements on our newsfeeds and even when we're genuinely thrilled for the happy couple, we still might wonder, *What if God is withholding this from me?*

Years ago, I found an article that went about as viral as articles could go in the early days of blogs. The author, a woman named Paige Benton who was single and worked in student ministry, wrote about the goodness of God and how His character does not change. Therefore, God is as good today as He will be tomorrow as He was yesterday. Based on this premise, she writes:

> I long to be married. My younger sister got married two months ago. She now has an adoring husband, a beautiful home, a whirlpool bathtub, and all-new Corningware. Is God being any less good to me than he is to her? The answer is a resounding NO. God will not be less good to me because God cannot be less good to me. It is a cosmic impossibility for God to shortchange any of his children.[1]

I know this is a lot easier said than done, especially when we are so deep in the muck that we don't know how to get back out without creating a mess. After all, grief has a tendency to be expressed as anger or bitterness or cynicism, and it almost always comes out sideways.

Because we're humans! With emotions! And sometimes our emotions take over! There are times when we are just too tired of fighting for light, and we allow our understandable feelings to turn into inappropriate outrage or jealousy or unkindness. If my feelings about singleness are leading me to believe that someone else is smaller than me or worth less than me or I use it to justify being unkind toward them even in my own mind, I need to slow down again.

Yes, someone else has something you want. However, their life circumstances do not directly influence your relational status. The fact of the matter is that someone else getting engaged does not indicate your unworthiness to be loved. Someone else being in a relationship is not a reflection of your unmarriageable character. Someone else having a child is not proof that you are not seen by God.

If looking at a photo of someone getting engaged or married or what have you is something that can be triggering for you, maybe the best thing you can do is mute them for a moment or scroll past and take a break. Have some grace for yourself as you navigate different experiences and levels of lament.

If Jesus can make room for feeling the loss of Lazarus, we can make room for letting ourselves honor and experience our emotions.

One of the very best things I've done with my twenties and thirties is regularly see a therapist. There are big "T" traumas that I have worked through and found healing from, but there are also a lot of little "t" traumas that a therapist is trained to walk us through as well. The very best people I know who have had the most steady and grounded outlooks have almost always been people who regularly take time to slow down and process with a counselor.

Yes, Jesus is enough. But He also gives us food to eat and professionals to help us and allows us to live in a time when medication is readily available. You do not have to do this alone, and commiserating in a healthy way can mean asking for help and receiving it.

God, in His kindness, encouraged my counselors and countless others to go to school and learn about how the mind works, so they can sit across from people like you and me and help us untangle our emotions and access the tools we need to live in a way that is healed and whole—a way of true shalom that can ultimately be found in the Jesus who stood beside Mary and Martha, weeping.

My friend Sandra has a song called "I Can't Help Myself" in which she recognizes that there is no way she can be her own savior. It's based on Psalm 121:1–2: "I lift up my eyes to the mountains—where does my help come from? My help comes from the LORD, the Maker of heaven and earth."

Beyond being all-powerful, God is also a good Father who is interested in what His children say, and we can bring Him our burdens. In the song, Sandra sings,

> Trust the Lord, my soul and all that is in me
> Oh, trust the light to show your darkest parts
> With wounds of truth and love, a friend who has known me
> A fool would keep his secrets in his heart[2]

When I leave my struggles and my cynicism in the dark, they can be fed and turned into something that takes over much more of my life than is healthy. I can easily give in to hopelessness, but when I commiserate with others, I am reminded of the bigger picture.

God can be sovereign, and I can be struggling. I can trust that He has things in control, and I can also feel sad that I don't know what in the world is going on. I can believe the best about God even on days when I'm worried about the worst-case scenario. We are human beings with a full spectrum of emotions, and part of living in a broken world with unmet hopes is recognizing that this is complex.

There will be days when singleness feels like freedom. And there will be days when it feels like a bad dream, and you're left sitting up in the darkness, wishing for the ache to subside. You are not alone in your wandering and watching and waiting. And you don't have to go it alone either.

We desperately need others to remind us of what is true on the days when we cannot believe it for ourselves. Like a text with a heart emoji on a random Tuesday morning, Jesus has given us the gift of one another, and it makes all the difference. Lean into your community when you are in a season of cynicism and lament. Open your mouth and tell others what is going on in your head and heart.

If someone knows that weddings are tricky for you, maybe ask them to sit next to you during the ceremony. If someone is aware that your week has been filled with rejection or loneliness, let them know to check in on you. If you're not sure where to start or what you're even needing, slow down and feel your feelings, letting them remind you that Jesus is ready to commiserate with you.

We are made by a commiserating God to turn to others and ultimately to God Himself in order to feel seen and cared for. He enters the mess and says, "Wow. This is a mess." He doesn't try to sugarcoat or hand you a trite phrase. No, He tells us what is truly happening—the good, hard, and vulnerable. And He sees what is true, even when we can't.

Sometimes I get stuck in my head, and when I do, I can forget what is true. My mind tells me a story that seems very accurate but is skewed by my own perspective and my own biases and my own insecurities.

Give me enough time and I can forget that anyone is in my corner.

I noticed this tendency a while back, so I started asking friends to preach truth to me and keep me grounded when anxieties or assumptions want to rule the day.

Some of the best decisions I have made in my relationships involve me explicitly asking people to step in with a pair of bolt cutters and unlock me from my own self-sabotage and desire to isolate. There are people in my life who I trust, and I can go to them and ask them to tell me the truth, and they actually will. They have the ability to step in and remove me from myself. In love, they tell me that I might be wrong, or maybe I need a break, or my feelings are valid but they do not get to make my decisions.

Who are the people in your life you can hand the bolt cutters to? Who are the people you can ask to kick in the door and bring you back to the table? If you know someone who has been trustworthy, let them know what they mean to you. Ask them to intentionally journey with you through your lament.

And if you aren't sure that you have those people? Pray and ask the Lord to strengthen the relationships you have and bring people into your life who can help in this process.

Perhaps there's a mentoring program at your church that you can sign up for to receive counsel from someone wiser than you. Or maybe there is a person in your community who you really admire and you can ask to meet once a month for coffee.

This is what I know from my very limited understanding at thirty-five years old: There are healthy and unhealthy ways to wait on the Lord. There are healthy and unhealthy ways to ask for support. There are healthy and unhealthy ways to bond with others. There are healthy and unhealthy ways to exist in our communities. Each of us has the choice to invest wisely where we put our resources and our efforts.

You are not alone in your quest to be whole and held, and you are made in the image of a God who is always ready to hear and listen and answer your cries for help. He surrounds you with people on purpose, and it just might carve a way to wholeness.

three

Connection

I grew up on the West Coast, where hardly any home is more than one hundred years old, but when I moved to Massachusetts, that changed. It's not uncommon to find yourself in buildings that are over a hundred years old and have stood since before electricity and central air were commonplace. These old homes are beautiful and—without the intervention of air conditioning—when the weather is warm, the walls and the floors get nice and warm and the humidity brings to the surface a very distinct scent that is almost impossible to pull apart from a summer breeze. I'm not entirely sure when the humidity arrives, but it seems to show up strongly for several months before quietly making its exit.

Autumn in New England blows in with gold and orange as the sky turns a new shade of blue. It is cooler and brighter, and it almost feels like I am a child being distracted by a parent trying to take something from me. While I look up at the colors, feeling the crispness of a new season in the air, I am too distracted to notice that the moisture is leaving. Suddenly, we don't have the all-too-familiar humid mornings and afternoons. I start to need to sleep underneath my quilt again.

My days and nights dry out in such a subtle way that really only my hair can tell as it calms down from the summer frizz. And without realizing what's really happening, without registering too much of a shift in the temperature and humidity, I think nothing of it as I shuffle across the living room in my wool socks, reaching for the light switch as the sky has grown dark after dinner. And then I hear a sharp and quiet snap that causes me to whip my hand back and turn in surprise. It's happened to me hundreds of times before, but the very first time after months of not experiencing the jolt comes with an eyebrow raise of surprise.

The static building up in me found grounding and made connections.

I suppose this is what we mean when we say we felt a spark upon connecting with someone else. We reach out and expect a simple touch only to be met by a surprise and a bit of a pulse. But here's the funny thing about connection: You don't even have to make contact. You only have to get close before the spark jumps out to meet you.

If the start of any relationship is a spark, there has to be a buildup to get it to combust.

You have to shuffle across the living room in socks or slide your hand over a balloon or shift around in a leather seat in the car. This anticipation stores up energy in us, and as single people, we often spend more time storing energy than feeling the connection it leads to.

Each morning, I pull back my covers and swing my legs over the side of the bed, hovering above the rug. Morning light makes the dawn feel a little kinder in a quiet house. One last reach up to the sky provides a good stretch, and, shaking it all out, I exhale before planting my feet. After slowly standing, I move forward, building static.

And the days go on and the nights continue the movement, building and building, but never getting quite close enough to hit a connection and feel the zap. Over time, the memory of connection feels far away. And on my darkest mornings, I'm not sure I remember what it felt like to connect at all.

There's not one specific moment when a lack of connection started. We are not vacuum cleaners with only one on-off switch and a cable connected to prongs that can be inserted into the wall wherever an outlet might happen to be. No, the connection points necessary to our survival are legion.

We don't just need one hug at church on Sunday or eye contact at brunch on Saturday morning. We don't just need one encouraging text message or one long drive to see something beautiful. No, we need a thousand tiny points of connection, each contributing to our well-being. As adults, it feels almost childish to say that we *need* connection. It feels juvenile to ask for someone to give us a hug or to see us or to offer what feels like a rudimentary sense of belonging. But the truth is, we were made from the very beginning to have connection because it is something that our God has based every relationship on.

I have an affinity for incorporating the story of Genesis into my books because I believe that if we want to know how we got to this particular day, we have to go back to the very beginning. I'm sure that the story of Genesis 1 and the origins of humankind are familiar to many, so I offer you this summary: There was nothing, and then, God made something. In fact, He made a whole lot of somethings.

And each of those somethings had a somewhere to belong. Each new day of the creation story, God begins by making a place, a home, for some creature or thing. And once He makes the sky and the land and the sea, He fills them up with inhabitants. This is a very distinct pattern that He sets forth: home-making and home-filling.

The vast expanse of the sky is filled with birds. The rolling hills and shorelines are populated by animals that walk and crawl and climb. The deep and mysterious sea is filled with fish and sea creatures, some of which to this day have never been discovered or fully understood. The world is teeming with plants and animals and beauty and goodness. And then, God decides that His grand finale will be humankind.

What I find interesting is that God does not tell us anything about the temperament of the creatures. He doesn't mention that the birds were free and happy or that the fish were content. He only says that they exist. But when He creates humans, He makes it known that He has concern for their relational state. It is not enough for them to have a home; that home must be filled. So when God makes Adam and breathes life into his newly formed lungs, He does not only hand him food to eat or fire to provide warmth or a shelter to protect him. No, He decides that Adam needs connection: "Then the LORD God said, 'It is not good for the man to be alone. I will make a helper corresponding to him'" (Gen. 2:18 CSB).

Woman enters the picture because it is not good that the man is alone. Both of them need companionship, but it begins with connection. They are not merely good friends who enjoy the company of one another. They are not simply coworkers who have a duty to team up and accomplish tasks. They are not solely lovers who only use their bodies to fulfill every pleasurable desire. No, they are connected down to their souls because their cores were made by a Triune God who values relationships.

God Himself is described as three in one. This mysterious way of existing has confounded and inspired theologians and artists for millennia. He is three persons: Father, Son, and Holy Spirit. Within these three persons is one perfectly united God. The Father is not the Son, and the Son is not the Spirit, and the Spirit is not the Father. Each of Them brings something unique to the table and to the Trinity. At the same time, They work completely connected to one another. Jesus, when He comes in the form of flesh to Earth, is not on a heavenly side quest. No, He is doing the work of the Father with the help of the Holy Spirit. They are united in mission, work, and being. Some say a better word for the Trinity would be *Tri-Unity*.

You see, the God we serve is not only into unity and relationships and connection—it is His very way of existing in the world we know and in the heaven we will know. Everything that God does is a relationship. So much so that He decides to make man and woman in His image, meaning there are parts of us that reflect who He is. We will never be God, but we were made to reflect pieces of Him to the world around us.

There are qualities that God carries that we cannot, such as being all-knowing or all-powerful, but there are also attributes that we *can* experience in part, such as beauty and justice and goodness. On this side of eternity, we only know them in part, but when we encounter a hint of God-given connection, it is enough to cause us to pause and look up. It is a jolt at our fingertips as we cross from the living room to the kitchen, wrapped in a quilt, reaching for the light.

The shock of connection is felt few times more sacred than at the birth of a child.

The first time my sister went into labor, I was in the room. Ever a firstborn, my niece decided to arrive just before her due date, early enough to be polite. I was in Bible college and had a paper due, so I had stacks of books about Romans sitting in the corner of the delivery room while we waited for little Emma to make her grand appearance. None of us really knew what to expect, with this being the first child in the next generation, but my sister patiently bore out the hours and hours of labor with breathing and shifting around until it was finally time to bear down and welcome new life into our family.

As I stood by my sister's head and she pushed for what simultaneously felt like forever and hardly any time at all, I didn't know where to focus. I was used to taking photos, and my Nikon felt like an extension of my arm, but in that moment, there were two people who were so tied up in one another that I didn't know if I should home in on my sister or her daughter. It didn't really matter where I *thought* my focus should go because, just before midnight, the very instant Emma came out into the light and started crying that newborn, gasping cry, we all lifted our heads and burst into involuntary tears. The sound of a newborn cry has a way of pulling at our insides and instincts, and there is absolutely no resisting a response. When a new life makes itself known, heart-led movement takes over, and we come undone.

In the flurry of completing the labor process, there are a lot of moving parts, but one that I have always seen happen right away is that a nurse or doula takes the brand-new baby and carries them to try and connect them with their mother. In the hours and days that follow, skin-to-skin contact is not only common but encouraged as a way of bonding a child to their parents. This practice is not sentimental but scientific. We are made to connect from the moment we enter this world. Even as we develop in utero, we are literally connected in the womb, and as soon as we become the smallest bit disconnected, we know. I studied this phenomenon and stumbled upon an article that explained:

> The 2016 Cochrane Review supports using immediate or early skin-to-skin contact to promote breastfeeding. Advantages for the mother include earlier expulsion of the placenta, reduced bleeding, increased breastfeeding self-efficacy and lowered maternal stress levels. It has been suggested that the rise in the mother's oxytocin during the first hour after birth is related to the establishment of mother–infant bonding. Advantages for the baby include a decrease of the negative consequences of the "stress of being born," more optimal thermoregulation, continuing even in the first days and less crying.[1]

The stress of being born is traumatic for all involved. A mother's body goes through so many different shifts during the process of labor and delivery, and it takes months, if not years, to recover fully. The child has to adjust to life outside the womb, and both are left reeling a bit from the whole process. It makes sense that they keep reaching out for each other, aching for connection as if their well-being depends on it.

As I read further, I found this very interesting excerpt:

> If separated from their mother, babies exhibit a distinct separation distress call. This separation distress vocalization in mammalian species that stops at reunion may be nature's way of keeping newborn infants warm with maternal body temperature. The baby's call at separation is thus a survival mechanism.[2]

This is what I can't get over: when a baby begins crying because they are separated from their mother, they are not merely expressing emotional sadness or despair as I'd always assumed. Rather, the baby is using all of their physical strength to exert energy and stay warm. Crying out and making a fuss and shouting is a baby's way of surviving until they can be reunited with the warmth of their mother.

So often we judge people who desire connection, and we consider them to be clingy or infantile. But the truth is this: From the get-go, we were made to need and to be near others in relationship. In its purest form, connection is a beautiful and simple thing that allows two people to care for each other and be seen. It is not just to make a mother feel good or a baby feel satisfied; it is a need that we have been created to crave and it reflects the nature of our tender and caring God.

We often see connection as an added bonus, but what if it's for our survival? And what do we do when it feels like we're more disconnected than connected?

Whenever I go on social media and ask unmarried people the ways that they feel the least connected, it almost always has to do with feeling othered. Because we are single, we often don't get invited out with couples, or we can't join certain small groups when they are designed for married individuals. Churches have a tendency to divide up their ministries into what they call "life stages," but more accurately, they are dividing their ministries into relationship statuses. Singles ministry. Married ministry. Family ministry. Kids ministry.

There may or may not be a resource for you if you find yourself single in a local church. Many churches prioritize married ministry over single ministry, which means that when you are looking for opportunities to connect to the community of your local church, they may or may not actually exist. In an effort to make small groups welcoming to people coming from different perspectives, we've accidentally alienated single people in the local church.

Yes, there is a very large percentage of people in this world who are married or have children, but that means that single people become a forgotten minority, even though we still make up a pretty large percentage of the local church. It's not like one in two hundred people is single. No, accounting for divorce and the death of a spouse, there are a lot more single adults in our congregations than we realize. According to Barna Research, 31 percent of churchgoers are single.[3]

I deeply love my local church, but I also always have been discouraged by the reality of how isolating something as beautiful as the church can be. In theory, we belong in the pews, and we should be able to connect with like-minded friends and build relationships around our shared love of

Jesus. But a lot of the time, we walk into church on a Sunday, and we don't know where to sit or who to sit with. We listen to announcements about upcoming family events and marriage retreats, and we are surrounded by the reality that we do not fit into those particular demographics.

I am not suggesting that having a ministry for children or families is not important, but we have to consider that putting too much focus on our differences unintentionally carries the consequence of pulling single people apart from the fabric of our church. We already know that we wake up alone and can go for days without physical touch and that we eat our meals by ourselves unless we make intentional efforts and plans to be with others. We already know that if something were to happen to us, the emergency contact in our phones does not share our last name unless it is a parent or sibling. We are well aware of our singleness, and when we feel singled out because of the way that churches try to connect people by creating specific ministries, it can unintentionally add insult to injury.

In a society that feels more connected than ever, it is a heartbreaking truth that single people feel more *disconnected* than ever when they walk through the doors of their churches. I am certain that this is not done intentionally, but nevertheless, the fallout is this: Walking into the Lord's house should feel like home for anyone who is seeking God, but it's starting to feel like we're walking into someone else's home—someone who has a partner and a built-in support system under their roof. To put it another way, without us even trying or being aware that it's happening, little by little we stop feeling like we're on the home team and we become visitors.

Social situations can be exhausting, so let's step back and think about what it means to be social to begin with.

According to the American Psychological Association, *social* can be defined as "relating to the interactions between individuals, particularly as members of a group or a community."[4] This definition is helpful because it reminds us that it is not just about the outcome of an interaction but the nature of the interaction itself. The interaction is a point of connection that has a catalyst and a consequence.

When two people come together, it is not enough for them to exist in the same space. They have to legitimately interact with one another in order to be connected socially. In order to be part of a true social interaction, there must be others who are like us, and we need to find some commonality with one another. Groups or communities often have similar purposes or goals or visions. Each point of connection makes the relationship stronger. Each interaction is a bond that allows us to flourish.

In Scripture, when God established His nation in the people of Israel, He was not merely gathering individuals but placing them in a social setting in which they would have to interact with Him and with one another to build something good.

Remember: Our God is a very social God.

My friend Savannah is a licensed therapist, and once when we were discussing this very topic, she said, "The key to connection is proximity."

We cannot build a proper connection if we don't have proximity. In fact, there are a whole lot of ways that we believe we are connecting to people when we are not. As I unpacked this idea of proximity with Savannah, one of the first things she brought up was social media and how it leads to disconnection.

Signs of disconnection are anxiety, depression, and isolation, but we often get there one little bit at a time. The fact of the matter is we often ask ourselves when we got so numb or sad or isolated, but it's almost always a slow roll.

This is why we need to regularly check our connections and make sure we're in a healthy place and headed in a good direction. Notice that you're feeling more cynical or isolated? Consider spending time with an actual friend. Ask someone to grab dinner or brunch. See if there's a local event like a farmers market or art fair and wander around, processing the week. Whether the plan is organized or not, you have to reach out and make a connection.

There have been countless times I was ready to fall apart and a conversation with a friend pulled me out of my funk.

We are meant to experience life and relationships firsthand, not by extension. So while social media is not a bad thing in and of itself, we have to be realistic about what it is doing to our brains.

To be aware of something in theory is not the same as being there in the flesh, smelling the smoke from a campfire and holding on to the sleeve of a friend as you tell an exciting story. So when those photos come across our feed and we see what is going on, we are cognitively aware of it, but we are not truly *living* it. And the joy we experience over someone's big announcement can mask the complicated underbelly of other feelings that are also rising to the surface.

When we see someone's photo on social media, we often like it or feel a positive emotion because we care about that person. Maybe my friend Shelley is having a birthday party, and I'm so excited she is being celebrated. I see her surrounded by friends and I click the like button, and as I scroll from image to image after that, I see other similar posts.

Someone had a baby! Somebody just got engaged! Someone got a promotion!

All of these moments are celebratory or at least noteworthy, but what I don't realize is that the positive emotions that I am associating with these photos are not actually happening to me. I'm just seeing them unfold on a screen. I'm not hugging someone's kid at graduation, I'm not singing "Happy Birthday" with a crowd, and I'm not standing on the beach and witnessing someone get down on one knee.

And further, I am so happy for my friends, but it doesn't mean I'm not also sad.

Savannah explained that when we engage with social media, it masks the other complex emotions we may be feeling. When someone has a baby, we feel happy but also sad that we haven't gotten to hold that kid yet. Or when someone gets engaged, we feel happy for them, but sad about the current state of our love life. Or perhaps we're in the middle of a job search and we see that someone else just got that promotion, and now we feel even farther behind.

It seems that we've been nursing our wounds with sandpaper, believing that we are building connection when we're really robbing ourselves of it. We don't know what we don't know, so it's time to ask: How do we reconnect?

True connection involves being near someone and experiencing something for ourselves. Not just looking at photos or reading captions, not just hearing about it from someone else. No, if we want to connect with people around us, we have to make the effort to get together. Perhaps that sort of commitment isn't hard to make because you're a fairly extroverted or active person. But have you considered that others might do well when they're invited in? Or some might be stuck at home, unable to engage constantly with the world around them? At times, we have to go to others if we want to be good friends.

Sometimes, reaching out to build a new friendship will go well, and other times there may be moments of awkwardness or we'll say something we regret or we'll make a bad first impression. This is why we need a whole lot of grace for one another and for ourselves. Grace to give unmerited favor to those who let us down, and grace to remember that we are also still learning. All of us are still learning.

The truth is that people are busy, and we all have commitments or plans that we cannot move or things that come up at the last minute. Your friends are going to miss your call or they're going to have to decline an invitation, but that's not reflective of the value that you bring to the world. It's not fair for us to expect everyone to always say yes, and it can do more damage when we believe that it is.

"Sending a text to twenty people doesn't create connection. It's an illusion," Savannah said.

And she's right. According to research, "Social media has a reinforcing nature. Using it activates the brain's reward center by releasing dopamine, the 'feel-good chemical' linked to pleasurable activities such as sex, food, and social interaction."[5]

The technology we hold in our hands—from social media to the ability to call anyone at any time from any place—gives an illusion that people should always be accessible.

But in order to authentically connect, we have to be *inaccessible* to others.

You read that right. Here's what I mean: If I want to catch up with a friend during lunch, I need to flip my phone over or silence it or turn it off altogether. In order to be fully present where I am in real life, I need to not be constantly distracted. I have to know my actual human limits and spend my attention and time and effort like it's a finite resource. And that means that I'm going to miss calls, and I'm going to not always be immediately available to my friends.

Which is hard for all of us people pleasers. I want everyone to know that I care about them and would drop everything for them all the time. But if I'm going to drop everything, everything gets dropped.

In her song "The Bridge," Taylor Leonhardt sings, "It's not about what I'm keeping out, it's about what I'm keeping in."[6]

Knowing that we are limited in capacity and so are our friends is key to making connection work. We have to not just take a risk but calculate it. There well may be a cost to the risk of asking someone to get together or sharing something vulnerable.

What if they say no?

What if we grow apart?

What if they are unkind or tell me something hurtful?

And we have all been in these situations where an expectation or a hope for a relationship did not work out the way we anticipated. And whether our expectation was fair or not, it left us confused and discouraged and, if we're honest, bitter.

Still, to be fully known and to be truly known involves the risk of being exposed, and that means we have to show up as who we really are. We cannot always put our best foot forward; eventually we'll trip. And when we do, the person we're with is going to either respond in a way that will pull us together or tear us apart.

That is a scary reality, but the good news is that as we learn to be vulnerable in small ways, we can open up in bigger ways. No risk, no reward.

It is challenging but so very necessary to hold these tensions. We are hopeful but we are flexible. We want the best, but the worst thing might happen. We are going to extend invitations, but our friends may not be able to make it this time. We don't have the bandwidth for everything to be a yes, and others don't have the bandwidth either.

And that has to be okay, friend.

This is also a place where we can mend some of the relationships with our married friends specifically. Instead of taking so much personally, perhaps we can extend some kindness. They're trying to figure out how to do this married thing and make new friendships, and that means they might forget how to be gracious toward those of us who are unmarried.

Most married friends are trying to expand their social circles to other couples, and when we don't get invited, they aren't intending for us to feel left out. In fact, I believe that most people who invite only married friends to a gathering are probably thinking about their commonalities more than they are realizing our uninvited-ness.

How do we stop ourselves from pulling apart the fabric of our relationship as a reaction to them seemingly doing the same? How do we not respond to something discouraging by getting defensive or trying to discourage someone else?

Let's go back to that social study for a minute. As I waded a bit deeper into my study of social behavior, a word caught my eye: *prosocial*.

Prosocial is a word I had never encountered before, and it was described as "denoting or exhibiting behavior that benefits one or more other people, such as providing assistance to an older adult crossing the street."[7]

As I dug into prosocial behavior, it reminded me of how formative each social interaction can be. Every action or choice is either for or against building a healthy social structure. We are not passive in the ways that we engage with the world around us.

Therefore, when a Christian finds themselves on a social media platform or at a coffee shop or meeting someone for the first time, the question isn't about the interactions themselves, but how they choose to use them. When we are faced with a decision to include others or to do the hard work of building relationships even though we have been burned in the past, we can move in a prosocial direction by refusing to believe that all we are good for is neutrality or pulling apart.

It turns out that we cannot be neutral about relationship.

Thankfully, we have an example of prosocial behavior in the person of Jesus Christ. God has revealed Himself in many different ways throughout history, and the most effective possible way was for Him to enter into our human form. There is something powerful about Him being in a whirlwind or a burning bush, but there is something intensely comforting about a God who gets right down on our level to make eye contact with us.

For nine months, Mary is carrying Christ in her womb, feeling Him kick and shift around. She is keenly aware of His presence, and as He develops, it changes the way that she walks in the world. Her gait changes and her stamina shifts, and she feels the all-consuming work of growing a child in every moment. The idea that God could have shown up fully grown and with robes and parades but chose to enter in at our entry point is hard to grasp. The humility that He shows us is not only His own condescension but demonstrates to us His affection and His willingness to come alongside us *as one of us.*

Years ago, I sat in a seminary class where we were talking about the character of Jesus and the prophecies that He fulfilled in His appearance. I scribbled in the margin of my notes, "Jesus has to be who He is in order to do what He does." In order for Him to be a mediator, He has to enter in to the space of humankind while still being fully divine. In order for Him to see, He has to have eyes. In order for people to be healed by His touch, He has to have flesh. In order for us to understand His anguish on the cross, He has to have the full range of human emotion. What shocks us about the person of Jesus is not the tasks that He accomplishes as much as how He accomplishes them.

His story, right from the beginning, is about moving closer to us so that we can find peace, and He does so in a literal way at the start of the gospels.

Mary can feel a shift in her body. The transition from carrying to delivering. And it doesn't matter that she is not in the presence of an older, wiser woman who knows how this process goes; instinct is kicking in. Nothing is stopping this baby from showing up, even if it means showing up in a barn. She undergoes the stress of delivery and perhaps she had been prepared in some way previously by a mentor or by witnessing birth for other people, but now she's deep in it for herself and there's nothing quite like it. Every white-knuckle grip she has on Joseph's cloak and uncomfortable shift of her hips and back, trying to find a position that works, gives way to eventual relief. But that relief is not going to come without pain and struggle and, well, labor.

I wonder what sort of birthing plan Mary had prior to this moment. I wonder if she had previously planned to be with her mother or a close relative before she and Joseph were called to leave for Bethlehem. I wonder if, when she got the news that they would have to travel away from their home right at the time of delivery, she wept.

How would she do this without the women in her community?

After all, she, too, was made for community, and she was about to go through one of the most intense experiences known to a woman, without her support system.

As she bears down with energy that feels impossible to have, the Christ child finally is caught by Joseph and that cry—that tiny and helpless and gasping cry—fills the night and something in Mary comes undone. Joseph, still in shock and overcome by the power of childbirth and from witnessing the miracle of what has happened before his eyes, takes that tiny God-child and hands Him to His mother. Jesus is covered in blood and fluid and probably even some dust, given the surroundings. Mary is covered in the same dust and sweat and tears. And then, like generations before and generations after, they lie there, skin-to-skin, connecting. The violence of delivery gives way to the panting and sighing and exhaling of connection.

This is the mystery of being a human person: it takes struggle to end with connection.

Every argument that we settle and every beef that we squash and every awkward apology that we make can ultimately give way to connection. But when we feel uninvited or unseen, it's easy to try and remain numb or to protect ourselves by building walls.

I will never be vulnerable again.

The Prince of Peace Himself sees us slowly shuffling around and building up static, and He's ready to extend His mighty hand to ignite a spark. And this is what I love about Jesus: When He enters our lives, He brings comfort and He brings safety and He brings connection in a perfect way. We can move forward with confidence, following our human instinct to have close proximity, knowing that we will be embraced.

Unlike with our flawed human relationships, we don't have to worry about Jesus changing with the tides or having a bad day in which He treats us with contempt. No, He is always inviting us closer and meeting us with compassion and conviction, and He is not rolling His eyes at us. Connection with Christ is our truest home, and when we find confidence and belonging there, we can risk the potential rejection of getting too close to others because that rejection no longer has the final say.

When there is abundance, we can give freely.

All of us, married or single, have a need for connection. Our connected God desires to give us just that. And when we find our truest home in Him, we can exhale, stepping back into the world around us and the relationships before us with joy rather than measured testing and frustration. When our hope is not in the next invitation (or lack thereof), we can see others as very human humans, and it gives way to freedom.

Our truest connection is not with the women in our church or the friends who have gotten married over the years or the besties from college who are always going to meet up for that girls' weekend to recharge and catch up. No, all of these good and beautiful friendships will fail us at some point. But Christ—who came into the world with a spark of desire to be close to His mother and His father and His friends and His disciples—is the One who shows us a different way of existing that isn't based on what we bring to the table or what our relationship status is, but on the simple fact that we are human beings and we were made for connection.

You are not alone in your ache to feel connection with someone. You are not alone in your desire to feel the spark. And I promise you, friend, that your longings for these good, God-given things are not in vain. As we consider how to step forward together, my prayer is that we can do so remembering that God made us all to ache after these good things. He designed us to be part of community, and while that's gotten muddled over the years, not all hope is lost. Because here's what I have seen, even in dark days: Single people show up.

When I need a ride home from the airport, those who have experienced this conundrum in the past are the first to volunteer. When I get sick and I feel overwhelmed, those who have also been sick and alone are the first to ask if they can bring dinner or drop off tissues and cough syrup. And they do so with a fire in their belly because they once were trampled and, by the grace of God, got back to their feet to show people a better way of moving forward.

As Christians, we are called to be the ones who show others a different way, even when those others are within the church. As those made in the image of God, we have an opportunity to live relationally with intentionality and connectedness, even though we often feel uninvited or unseen.

This opportunity does not discount the pain we have felt, but it does remind us that our feelings of being on the outside are not the end of the story.

I once stood on a mountain in the Sierra Nevada in California, and my brother-in-law pointed out a watchtower on the adjacent peak. There are people who go to these high overlooks and their job is to watch for signs of forest fires. They are the eyes in the hills, and they prevent disaster.

Single men and women in the pews are like watchers who look out for what's on the horizon. We are the ones who see those who are often overlooked. We are the ones who tell truth to those believing that they're not cared for. We are the ones who see what others do not, and it is a gift that the church desperately needs. We see the smoke rising and call it out so that lives can be spared and further damage isn't done.

We need you to get over here and be who you are because only you can spot certain needs and take action to fill them.

I promise you: Your eyes on the horizon and your willingness to participate in connecting to the world around you blesses and builds up. Keep shuffling. Keep reaching out. Keep making connection.

four

Commitment

I didn't date in high school, really. But when I was in my twenties, I fell in love for the first time. My first serious relationship was one that started in autumn, and he showed up with love notes and creative choose-your-own-adventure dates. He held the door open, and on Valentine's Day, he made little origami hearts that he handed to me all day as little sweet surprises, pressing them into my hand when I wasn't looking.

And then, one night in the early spring, he told me that it was over. I was devastated.

I remember walking away from his apartment the night we broke up and feeling a deep ache, trying to catch my breath as I walked between the bare trees that hadn't grown spring leaves yet since they all fell in the fall when he was holding my hand and telling me he wanted me to be his girlfriend.

Five years later, I met someone new, and it was something out of a movie.

The scene was set: It was winter in New England, and he was a friend of a friend. I had a canceled flight because of a snowstorm that left me stranded another day in Boston, which gave us the chance to hang out. Things moved slower, but a few months later, after emails and friendship and chemistry, we decided to date.

It was long-distance, but we made it work with Face-Time and phone calls and plane rides. He started school in Boston, I would go visit for long weekends, and we would play board games and make dinner and go walking on the snowy marsh.

And then it happened again. Springtime. Again.

"I think we should break up."

I was left reeling, having fallen deeper for this man than the first. And I sat in my counselor's office and told her, "I just don't understand what I did wrong. We did everything I thought we were supposed to. We were friends first, we took things slow, it just made sense."

And isn't that the way it goes? It all makes sense until it doesn't anymore. Until one day, one of you says, "I just can't do this anymore."

And because you were only dating, you hadn't moved to a deeper partnership. But the planning of the future was there. The hope was there. The love—or at least the beginning of it—was there.

Wasn't it?

I caught these glimpses of love and then was left with empty hands time and again. I had connected the dots and felt the pull toward another person, imagining my whole future with them only to be left sitting by myself, very sad and wishing we were together again.

Love, it turns out, is not like a movie or a contest or a reality show. There are yeses and there are nos. There are dates and there are breakups. And nearly all of it truly is out of our control. We cannot get someone else to love us any more than we can will the rain to stop falling.

And the worst part is that you're not holding on to something that you once relied on. You can replay pivotal moments, but now they feel like they don't count. And the world moves on from your romance, but it sticks to you like tar. Someone goes from being so very close to being a distant memory.

But if I can be honest, I know—all these years later— exactly how it felt when he looked at me. I remember the curves of his handwriting and the feeling I would get every time my phone lit up with his name. Only instead of those images being something out of a dream, it feels haunting.

Both of those men married good women years ago now, but I have faced seasons and moves and job changes by myself.

How do we carry this tension as single people? How do we grow through our memories and become new versions of ourselves when past versions are tied to someone who isn't there anymore? How do we honor the person we were and still let ourselves become the person we're going to be? Being single is, at times, its own form of surrender, because anyone can decide they want to date you or no longer want to date you, so it's out of your hands.

I believe in the sovereignty of God, and I believe in His kindness and goodness. I believe that those men were the right ones at the right time, but we were not meant for one another in the end. I am not missing out on my life because I'm not with them. I have been sad that I did not have a partner, and I can still bless their marriages and pray that they thrive.

Sometimes, being single feels like being splintered into endless pieces. Like every heartache splits you a bit. Like every "I love you" that is taken back and every moment of tension leading to a breakup starts to unravel your steadiness. It feels like you'll never get past it until one day you wake up and you have a whole new life, and that person just isn't right in the middle of the mess anymore, and even though it once felt like an impossibility to move on, on you move.

Now I can say, on the other side of these breakups, that I am so glad we all ended up where we did. And I don't feel so very tender the way I did in those first weeks and months after those relationships ended.

When I think about the word *commitment*, a few different images come to mind, but the one that feels strongest is the image of walking away. Because I don't think we can talk about the part where someone stays until we process the part where someone left.

These moments are often unseen because we are out here trying to maintain some semblance of dignity and independence, and we don't want to be *that* person. We don't want to pine and ache and weep into the night. We don't want to come totally undone because that isn't how we made it this far as a single person. We made it this far by pulling our crap together and trying again, over and over. But this is the truth: Any romance, whether official or just a longing, does us in.

When the first ending settled into my heart, I was not well. No one prepares you for your first real heartbreak. For a few days, I tried the strong, silent approach, but finally a handful of girlfriends showed up one night to my house and they sat around in my room, which was entirely too small for that many people. For a few days, things felt steadier, but then my mood ebbed and flowed when he started dating again or when we shared classes or saw each other at friends' birthdays.

When the second heartache hit, I just didn't believe it was real. The denial route is always so dang inviting, right? And I wasn't the only one. Friends assured me that there was no way this was how it all ended. No one saw it coming. It was so sudden that it felt like a waiting game more than anything else.

Surely, he'd come back.

But as the weeks went on and stretched into months, I stopped praying every day for it to be untrue. And I had to do the work of walking away from the one who had already abandoned the effort of being an "us."

At thirty-five, I can tell you that the ache of someone not committing is one that lingers. Because this is the thing about commitment: It is hoped for but not always made. You live on this precipice of wondering if maybe someone will say, "Yes, I want this. I'm in." But a new year comes, and it still hasn't happened. Or maybe they did say it, but then those vows were broken.

People are wildly wonderful and also very much so human, leaving us desolate.

Each heartache scarred me, but it also reminded me that there are others who are ready to love us. Friends brought me different foods to try to get me to eat because I hadn't been able to. They swore up and down that he was an idiot. They told me I wasn't alone.

I still remember one of them took my ex-boyfriend's sweater and flannel shirt and anything else that was in sight and put it all in a box. She took it with her, declaring that if I wanted it back one day, I could have it, but I didn't need to sit with it. She helped me set down the burdens I didn't even know I was holding. This was my first glimpse of commitment not only being the exchanging of a ring, but the willingness to advocate and provide for another.

My friends preached to me that I was seen and loved by God and by them doing so, I was reminded that I was seen and loved by them too. Since then, several of these compadres have faced heartache of their own, and I've been able to show up or bring a meal or leave them a note.

See, we don't just want someone to commit to us, we want to commit to someone else too.

However you came into your singleness, you know the feeling of longing well. Even outside of dating, you know the feeling of wanting to call someone on a long drive home, only to be met with their voicemail. Or you get sick and there's no one who offers you their presence. There is no one who proudly bears the go-to role of caretaker.

What do we do with this? This longing and this ache to matter enough that someone commits? This hollow sort of feeling that suggests that no one owes us community?

I suppose the first thing we have to do is call it what it is: loneliness. When no one is there to commit to you, it feels very lonely. And we can be convinced that we're not just lonely, but actually alone.

Commitment

The Bible is full of lonely people, but the one who keeps coming to my mind is Hagar. She was a woman with no one to turn to who found herself before a God who commits.

Hagar was a servant of a couple named Sarai and Abram. Back then, having a child meant that your legacy was secure, but Sarai had a hard time having children. So Sarai offered her servant to her husband. Abram got Hagar pregnant so he would have someone to continue his line. Sarai was filled with anger and jealousy, so she abused Hagar, who fled into the wilderness. As a pregnant woman, Hagar had no one to defend her, but God showed up and told her that she would not have to do this alone.

She ended up returning to her home and later gave birth to a son—Ishmael (meaning "God hears").

After the child was born, Sarah also got pregnant and, having no real need of Hagar anymore, cast her out.

Once again, Hagar is on her own.

Here is Hagar, completely helpless. She has no employer, and she has no husband or family to care for her. After years of abuse and mistreatment, she is at the end of the line. She has been cast out with her son who is too young to fend for himself and she has no way of caring for him. She has run out of water in the desert, both figuratively and literally. And one day, as the temperature rises, she walks away from Ishmael, knowing that perhaps some distance will mean she doesn't have to watch him die:

> When the water in the skin was gone, she put the boy under one of the bushes. Then she went off and sat down about a bowshot away, for she thought, "I cannot watch the boy die." And as she sat there, she began to sob. (Gen. 21:15–16)

She is dying and she is weeping and all she can think to do is walk away to avoid watching her only son die in the barren land they've been banished to. I imagine that her lips were cracked and her tears dried up and her head was throbbing. When you live in the Middle East, you are used to the heat, but this is next-level. To get to this level of despair, things must truly be hopeless.

No one owed her anything.

No one was committed to caring for her.

No one was there to listen as she deliberated about what to do next.

She wasn't just backed into a corner—she was exposed to the elements.

God heard the boy crying, and the angel of God called to Hagar from heaven and said to her, "What is the matter, Hagar? Do not be afraid; God has heard the boy crying as he lies there. Lift the boy up and take him by the hand, for I will make him into a great nation."

Then God opened her eyes and she saw a well of water. So she went and filled the skin with water and gave the boy a drink. (vv. 17–19)

When Hagar could not lay eyes on her son or listen to his cries for a moment longer, God heard him. And when Hagar walked away so they wouldn't have to look at each other dying, God saw her. He provided for them and promised to care for them.

Hagar is the only person in Scripture to give God a name, and what she chooses is *El Roi*. The God who sees me. This woman who was overlooked and underappreciated was suddenly looked upon. This woman who was taken for granted and abused was suddenly noticed. This woman who was certain that death was coming for her and the person she loved most was suddenly seen.

When we are seen, everything changes.

And all of us have a need to be looked after. It's not only married people who understand the need for commitment and choosing another person. No, we all have that longing. We all want someone to initiate first and choose *us*. We all want someone to show up when we need it the most. We all just want someone to show up, even in moments when we don't think we need help.

Commitment is not just a promise but a presence.

It is a willingness to make sure that someone is not alone as they venture through life. When someone gets married and they commit, they are agreeing to be present and to not leave. They are agreeing to stay.

You need to know that you deserve to be seen and heard and you do not deserve to be left. Who you are on a basic level is a person made in the image of God, and God has made it *very* clear that He is committed to His people. So when you start to wonder if you are truly alone, the answer is a resounding *no*. Because you could be in the heart of the wilderness dying of thirst, and He would still hear you. You could be cast to the side and entirely rejected, and He would still see you.

Everyone's experience of the love of God is different, and He does not meet us all in the exact same way. But we can see His character in the stories of Scripture, and this story reminds me that my cries are never outside of the range of His hearing, and my tears are never too far away for Him to bear witness. In fact, Scripture tells us that He bottles our tears and counts them as something precious (Ps. 56:8).

In the ancient Near East, people carried around statues of their gods. They worshiped idols that they carved or made by hand. And when God Himself is written about in the Old Testament, He is contrasted with these idols who have eyes but do not see and ears but cannot hear (Ps. 135:16–17).

What makes Him stand out is the fact that He engages with His people. And through covenants, He promises Himself to them—and to us. Even when we fall short, He has mercy. Even when we forget who we are and who He is, God stays steadfast. If we are made in His image, we are made to reflect His character, and that character does not shy away from commitment.

Our God looks at us and says, "Yes, I want this. I'm in."

Did you know that you are not an afterthought to Jesus? Did you know that He knows the number of hairs on your head and was there knitting you together in your mother's womb? Did you know that He delights in you and sees you as a beloved child?

God commits to us over and over again. And then He invites us into the work of committing to others. We don't have to assume that we can't participate in a committed and faithful lifestyle or that we are exempt from committing to others because our God, who is all in on us, extends a call for us to live this way in our friendships and families.

We cannot control if someone is ready to commit to us, but we must be willing to start the conversation or at least go first. As intimidating as that can be, I have found that investing in friendships with no motivation for reciprocation allows me to love freely without expectation. It also allows me to learn how to trust that this life of committing is how I was intentionally wired, and each time I take the risk of trying to commit, I am being conformed more to the image of God, and I'm trusting Him with the outcome too.

Here are some ways to start moving toward a committed life:

1. Show up.

Perhaps the simplest but most overlooked way of committing to relationships is showing up. Return the text. Respond to the email. Invite them for dinner or even to run errands. If you don't set a pattern of showing up for people in the day-to-day, how will they know who to call when things go wrong and they're left needing support?

We don't find our people in our silos; we find them by putting in the hours of connection and presence. When we show up for one another, we communicate that our efforts are for their good and worth our while.

There's a song by Sara Groves in which she sings, "It will take days and days, and it might be extravagant and wasteful. But we'll be gone as long as it takes."[1] There is a certain wastefulness in the eyes of the highly logical when it comes to putting forth extravagant effort that may not be returned. Some might count the cost of time and say that it's not worth their while to show up. But I've never met someone who was disappointed that someone showed up to their art show or birthday party or wedding or parent's funeral. In an age of technology, we can give people our presence, and that is a gift that cannot be substituted.

2. Speak up.

Not everyone considers words of affirmation to be their love language, but everyone needs to be told that they are cared about. Sometimes we do that through our actions, and other times we have the opportunity to be straightforward and specific in our encouragement. When we lose someone we love, one of the hardest parts is the fact that we never get to talk to them again. We don't get to tell them how much we care or how grateful we are for their friendship.

Four years ago, I lost my dear friend Jill whom I had known since college. She was a joy and a delight, and after we moved away from the same town, it was easy enough to go months without catching up. We were young and living our lives, but when she got sick, we made it a point to talk more often. And now that she's gone, I still think about how much I wish I had told her more often what she meant to me.

A friendship will speak for itself in theory, but it's also a privilege that we get to speak truth and belonging and life over one another. When we commit our words to the building of relationships, we are doing more than we realize. We are giving voice to the thoughts that we have and the intentions that we carry. If you have the privilege of being alive at the same time as someone else, tell them how you feel about them and speak life and love over them, even if it's been a while.

3. Seek out.

The majority of my life, I have been fairly passive in how I interact with most people. I have my groups that I spend time with, but it's easy to feel like we don't need to make an extra effort with acquaintances or friends who we only see occasionally. While we only have so much bandwidth and cannot be close to every single person, I also think we can be intentional with how we interact with those around us. We can still shoot a quick text to somebody and tell them we're thinking of them. We can still go out to coffee with a new person from church. We can still pursue relationships without spreading ourselves too thin.

Being pursued in friendship feels really good, but we often grow when we make it a point to pursue others as well. You have friends who are introverted or isolated or quiet, and you have the chance to welcome them in. We've all been in that position of being too overwhelmed or uncertain or exhausted to reach out. Have compassion for one another and pursue friendship without keeping score.

I think about the parable of the wedding feast in Matthew 22. A man is throwing a banquet and invites all of the most popular people, but none of them come to the party. And then, because the party is set, the man decides to invite everyone else. He sends servants down the street, grabbing anyone who will listen to his invitation, and they have a feast together. This is a beautiful example of welcoming those who you might not think to invite at first glance. But they deserve to feast as well. They deserve to be invited in as well. They deserve to be pursued as well.

Part of being a committed person is committing yourself to whatever builds community.

It's about carrying a willingness to keep coming back to what is going to cultivate good and beautiful and necessary things. And while it can feel like work at times, there are also times that it can feel like freedom. Like when the first tomato turns red on the vine, and we forget that we ever struggled to be a gardener. We can freely commit because we trust that there is something good on the other side. Like following our GPS when we can't see exactly where it's going to lead, we can commit to the next right turn, trusting it's going to move us one step closer to the destination we're bound for.

And this is why we need to have grace for ourselves. Because sometimes? We move forward in a relationship and then realize that this isn't going to end the way we thought. And that's okay. When a romantic relationship ends, we can heal and move forward. But it doesn't mean that our willingness to commit or the risks we took in that relationship were simply not meant for us. We might not be meant to be with that person, but we're still meant to commit to relationships on the whole (Gal. 6:2; Rom. 12:15).

For every relationship that has slipped through the cracks, I have been held by a God who does not disappear like a mist. For every moment of abandonment, I have been met by a God who keeps His promise not to forsake me. I keep looking up, and He keeps still being there. And for every moment of wondering if Christ will provide a way through heartache, I have been carried by Him and His people. I am a woman who is committed and committed to by the grace of God and the people of God.

We don't know much more about Hagar after she is met by God. But we know that God kept His promise to save not only her life but also her son's life. Though she was a woman who was not married, she knew the goodness and fullness of commitment. She experienced the rich nature of our faithful God just as much as anyone else.

The same is true for you, friend. You are not doomed to a life of no commitment. In fact, you can look around and see traces of it everywhere. In your friend's marriage vows, sure, but also in the way that small groups meet regularly and coworkers share meals. In regularly texting to check in with loved ones and creating long-standing traditions like girls' weekends or birthday meals.

Showing up and saying, "Yes, I want this. I'm in" is what you were made to do.

five

Communication

"*I think that there's been* a miscommunication."

We sat there over tacos and queso, and Shauna looked at me with a soft, knowing smile on her face and her eyebrows raised. Ever the kind-hearted confidant, Shauna has a way about her that allows me to be totally straightforward. I had just told her about how I was almost certainly being abandoned by my friends. The irony of sitting with beloved friends and telling them I'm feeling friendless is embarrassing, but I was so stubbornly sure that a recent dry spell in some of my relationships was not my fault.

This had to be on them.

There's no way I could have communicated anything but friendship and invitation. I believe I did everything right!

Let's be real, though: Shauna was the one who was right.

When friends grow apart for a season, it's often a two-way street.

"Is it possible that you've communicated to them that you want space?"

It was totally possible.

"No," I said.

She sat patiently.

The perceived distance I was feeling with a friend group could have come from the fact that I'd been sick for two weeks and also traveling and also overscheduling. Of course I was feeling friendless; I couldn't seem to find any margin to nurture my friendships.

Finally, after over-defending myself, I said, "You know, I suppose it's possible that maybe, just *maybe*, we're all a bit busy and it's not personal."

Of course, I had spent the entire previous weekend telling myself it *was* personal, and these pals *didn't* want to be my friends anymore. I had entire conversations in my mind and had created some kind of reality in which they just did not care anymore. Even though we'd been friends for years. Even though we'd all been going through some transitions and new schedules.

Here's the thing about imaginary conversations: They are very convincing, and we always end up winning those arguments in our minds. But here's the other thing: If you have imaginary conversations, you're also building imaginary friendships.

Almost always, an imaginary conversation does not benefit the real-life person in front of you. In fact, it turns them into a silenced, objectified entity. I know that sounds really harsh, but let's unpack it.

There are two ways that we can see people: We can see them as humans with diverse wants and needs and experiences, or we can see them as a set of ideas or a representative of a position. We can remove them from their true state of complexity and nuance, and we can put them into categories. While this may be easier for conversations that we like to have in our head, it's also a wildly unfair way to view another person.

Consider the alternative. What if you apologized to someone, and they responded with grace instead of condemnation? What if you brought up your thoughts and they agreed with you instead of pushing back? As humans, we are unpredictable and constantly changing. This is one of the things that makes us different from God, who never changes.

When you approach conversation with a human person, there is an element of surprise because you just never know how they might respond. Sometimes, it's a disaster. But there are also moments when it goes better than expected. And the only way to figure out how a situation will unfold is to walk in, open your mouth, and communicate properly.

Easier said than done.

People often say that the key to success in any relationship is communication. And beyond a general consensus, we are created by a relational God, and His triune nature gives us a perfect example of unity and connection, so it's important that we value communication.

As we talked about with Genesis 1, the world is quiet and void, and then, out of that darkness, God speaks. He could have just created with a snap or a thought, but instead, He chose to use words. When He spoke, His words gave way to creation. His very manner of making things is to *speak* them to life.

As the Old Testament unfolds, He makes Himself known in miraculous and straightforward ways. He calls prophets and priests and kings, freaking them out because of the intensity of His unexpected message. Most of the time when God reaches out to someone, they are in disbelief. He sends angels or messengers to relay His information just to ease the blow of how incredibly intense it is when He speaks.

These messengers bring good news, rough news, warnings, and direction, and even *their* presence is intimidating. Then, they announce the coming of Jesus, and when He arrives, the Gospel of John tells us Jesus is *the Word made flesh*: "In the beginning was the Word, and the Word was with God, and the Word was God. He was with God in the beginning. Through him all things were made; without him nothing was made that has been made" (John 1:1–3).

Our God values words and is Himself revealing His character through His Word, and Jesus is known as *the Word* for a reason. It is not a mystery how God feels about words. And His words are true and clear, but ours get muddled when we try to use them.

As fallen beings, we are marked by sin and a dark world, and we often use words to hurt or manipulate or coerce or abuse. We have the opportunity to use our language and communication for the good of others, reflecting the heart of God, and yet in our sinful nature, we can choose to change them into something damaging.

Look at the interaction that Eve has in the garden with the serpent in Genesis 3. In the very first opportunity he has to influence humankind and turn them against their Creator, Satan chooses to create confusion about what God has spoken. He asks the question, "Did He really say . . . ?" as a way of stirring division and doubt and trying to wedge something between humankind and a God who had clearly spoken to them with specific words and directions.

110

It does not surprise me that the first sin was committed as a result of the serpent's twisting of God's Word. We have been falling into this pattern since the very start. We are given clarity, and we turn it into confusion. We are given opportunities to exhort, and we choose instead to exhaust. Whether we intend to or not, we are regularly missing the point with our inability to communicate with clarity and kindness.

Many times, I have complicated my life by taking what God has said in Scripture and misinterpreting or misapplying it. I read that God is forgiving, but I believe that He wouldn't forgive me if He knew the things I thought when that person cut me off in that meeting. I read that God is patient, but I believe He's run out of patience with my stubbornness. I read that God is a provider, but I believe that I will run out of what I need and this next season is going to be one in which I just don't have enough.

The narratives that we tell ourselves have such a hold on us, right? We can open the Bible and read truth but not take it to heart. We are quick to believe that God is asking us to hustle or do things on our own strength or burn out for the kingdom, forgetting that He asks us to truly trust Him and have humility to know our limits and prioritize rest and the Sabbath.

God is not shocked. He knows us completely and He understands our nature and how we honestly cannot help ourselves. Whether we acknowledge His perfection in His communication or not, we are wandering around and bumping into these terrible habits of miscommunication along the way.

Jesus, who is God, is all-knowing. The word for this is *omniscient*. Still, knowing exactly what He was getting Himself into, He drew near to the disciples. He was well aware they would be fickle and grumpy and doubtful, but still, one day, He invited a fisherman named Peter to follow Him.

Peter was passionate and quick to jump to mostly wrong conclusions. Peter was often the first to volunteer or talk about how much faith he had and what a good disciple he was, but when the pressure showed up, he struggled to follow through. When he walked on water to Jesus, Peter started to look away from Jesus and his faith withered and he began to sink. He was so certain that he was set apart from his peers, but he regularly jumped in too quickly and couldn't stay faithful to the ways of Jesus.

Jesus knew that this facade would not hold up, and yet He did not constantly stop Peter from people-pleasing. He knew that Peter was going to deny that he even knew Him, and yet Christ offered him bread and friendship, over and over again. There was never a moment that Jesus backed away from Peter, even though Peter had shown himself to be very concerned about the wrong things.

One spring evening, everyone is taking their place at the Passover feast. Candles are flickering, an elaborate meal is served, and for a moment, all are together one final time before Jesus's arrest, and Peter proclaims that there is no way that he would ever betray Him. The two of them lock eyes, and Peter's earnest expression is met with absolute heartache. Surely Jesus swallowed sadness as they dined and He knew what was coming next.

Hours later, the authorities arrest Jesus and He is carried away and the disciples scatter into the night. Peter finds himself watching from a short distance, gathered with others around a coal-burning fire in a courtyard.

"Hey, don't you know Jesus of Nazareth?"

"I swear I saw you with him recently."

"You seemed close."

Close from years of companionship and travel. Close from shared meals and wearisome journeys. Close from homesickness and doubt and misunderstanding. Close from countless conversations and goodnights and see you laters.

"No," he says, "I don't know what you're talking about."

Jesus communicates constantly to Peter about how much He cares, but when the moment arrives for Peter to be loyal, he just can't muster it because he gets in his own way. His fear of rejection or even meeting the same fate as Christ is too much pressure, and he collapses.

All four gospels tell the story of Peter's denial in similar terms, except for Luke. He makes sure to add one small detail that until recently I'd overlooked. After the third denial,

> Peter replied, "Man, I don't know what you're talking about!" Just as he was speaking, the rooster crowed. The Lord turned and looked straight at Peter. Then Peter remembered the word the Lord had spoken to him: "Before the rooster crows today, you will disown me three times." And he went outside and wept bitterly. (Luke 22:60–62)

One commentator writes, "Luke had not told his readers that Jesus was anywhere near Peter. Perhaps Jesus was visible through a window, or His guards may have been leading Him past a place where He could see Peter. Luke's unique reference to His turning and looking at Peter adds to the shock effect of the moment."[1]

This moment of Peter's denial not only being witnessed but witnessed by Jesus Himself feels like a punch to the gut.

It sucks the air out of the room. They make eye contact and Peter is undone. I wonder if in that moment, he flashed back to hours earlier when Jesus was looking at him across the dinner table.

Soon, Jesus hangs on the cross, covered in His own blood, completely abused and depleted. He speaks nothing but compassion to the very end and then He breathes His last. On top of the grief of losing a friend, Peter is now facing deep regret and weeping bitterly because Jesus saw it all happen. He knows exactly what he has failed to do, and it will haunt him, especially in these early days after the death of Jesus.

I'm certain Peter was thinking, *There's no way I can recover from this.*

• • • •

Peter was heavy-hearted because he believed that even if Jesus really was going to rise from the dead as He'd promised, things would be different. Jesus wouldn't trust Peter again after what he'd said in those crucial moments when Jesus needed the support of His disciples more than ever. Peter had dropped the ball in the worst possible way, and I'm sure his mind was running away from him with a long list of reasons why Jesus was disappointed in him.

And isn't that the way it works? When something hard happens, we tend to go one of two ways: We either can't stop thinking about it, or we do everything we can to not have to think about it. Either I want to spin my wheels and hyperfocus on what I should have done differently or how I failed, or I want to go numb or pretend it never happened.

When we're feeling particularly vulnerable, it's easy to look for a distraction, right? We'd like to change the subject, hoping no one is noticing, and we won't have to move further into territory that feels too exposing. But when we shy away from acknowledging and communicating the truth of what we're walking through, we cheapen our friendships because we aren't building them on honesty.

And words left unspoken are a perfect opportunity for untruths to sneak in and tell us to believe that we're unloved and hopeless and never going to be candidates for good and healthy and hopeful friendships.

The truth is hard to swallow at times, but when we don't face it or talk it through, we're much worse off. We're left to fill in the blanks when information or context is missing. We go on assuming that if someone pulls back, they are not wanting to engage with us, when really they might be afraid to admit what's really bothering them. Or perhaps you've been in an unclear place with a friend where you can't read them or they can't read you, and both of you start to assume a motive or intention, which just hurts the relationship.

Many of our friendships fade and fizzle because of unspoken reassurances, apologies, and clarifications. We just go on assuming they meant to give us that info sarcastically or they must not want to hang out anymore, or perhaps we are waiting for them to pick up the phone and we don't want to go first. Forever in a stalemate, we miss out on one another.

As if it isn't already so easy to miss out on one another. With the addition of screens to conversation, we can all too readily pull out our cell phones, staring at screens when there are real live people in the room. I wonder if Peter would have rather been on his cell phone than admit his shame to others.

It seems to me that most of the time, we are at best only halfway present in our conversations. There's often a screen involved or a distraction or a loud atmosphere that is poking holes in the integrity of our conversations. One UC Irvine study found that it takes an average of twenty-three minutes and fifteen seconds to get back to a task once we have been interrupted.[2]

In this age of endless distraction, we're out here trying to communicate clearly, but wires are getting more and more crossed. We like to believe it's not so hard to do more than one thing at once, and we even tell ourselves we're doing those things well.

But I think we all know that it is impossible to do all of these things well. So here we are, attempting to have nuanced conversations with complex people, and we are confused when it doesn't go well or when miscommunication happens. Like having numb fingers and trying to find our car keys in the bottom of a cluttered backpack, we fumble around, making the best of a not-great situation.

We do not lament enough that the communication channels we have in this day and age have become rusted and tired. We are not good at being present or telling people how we feel on a regular basis. We are not consistent in overcommunicating our affection or hope or delight in one another.

Think about it: When was the last time you looked a good friend in the eye and thanked them for who they are and how they exist in the world? When was the last time you took a moment to express your love for someone in a quick text message or a note or a meal together?

It seems that we're just too busy to engage in meaningful ways because our affection and focus are being pulled in so many different directions. But here's the thing: If we want to engage authentically with our relationships, we have to

116

be able to push past the initial hurdle of pleasantries and distractions to get to the core of what's *really* happening. We have to face the uglies and scaries and uncomfies.

Fight to stay open and vulnerable with good friends. Don't offer your most tender stories and experiences to just anyone, but when someone is trustworthy? It's a good thing to communicate with them and tell them your story so they have context because it will lead to understanding that will build a better bond.

I have found that sharing a life story is daunting, but when I make the effort to explain some backstory here and there, my friendships are richer as a result. Is this easy to do? No. But is it necessary? I think so.

Our goal should be to be clear about where we're at. Passive-aggressive tendencies will wreck a friendship faster than nearly anything. But beyond conflict, we also have to be so, so clear about assuming the best because even great communicators can still misunderstand and be misunderstood.

I once asked some friends for help, and no one responded. I was sure my counselor would tell me they were the problem and it was their fault I was feeling unloved, and she simply and wisely said, "Ask again. It's not a sign you're unloved if someone can't show up. Hold a posture of gratitude and constant letting go of expectations. Everyone is always looking at someone or something else and we have to be mature and realistic."

She's not wrong. I was assuming the worst when I had not considered that in the same way that I feel pulled in thirty-five directions, my friends do too! Maybe someone read the text and intended to respond but their kid spilled their lunch and they had to set down their phone and help.

Maybe another friend wished they could show up but their schedule just won't allow it. There are so many good and understandable reasons to drop a ball, and we need to have grace for it.

Still, misunderstandings erode what can already feel shaky, and as single people, we are often feeling uneasy around communication because a lot of the time people say one thing and do another. They say that they want to get together and yet they keep only hanging out with married people. They proclaim that they are supportive of their single friends, but they don't take the time and effort and energy to understand our perspective. When relationship status does come up, it feels like many are quick to try and problem-solve rather than listen and try to understand.

This can be *exhausting*.

Where do we begin? This Mount Everest of figuring out healthy communication can feel overwhelming. So let's slow down and start by opening our mouths and telling the truth instead of having those imaginary conversations that are only adding to the chaos.

Consider this: What would happen if we reached out to a close friend who we haven't talked to in a long time and apologized for being distant? What if we told them how much we missed them or what we miss the most about them? Or what if we just reached out to friends we *do* see often and told them that we love being their friend?

It's been years since my friend Jill died, and I still regularly dream about her or wish that I could have made better use of the time we had together. After college, we very naturally drifted apart the way that people do in their early twenties. And by the grace of God, we came back together when things started to get very intense around her cancer diagnosis, but there were still those years in between that felt lost. I would do almost anything to be able to pick up my phone right now and shoot her a text or a funny meme, but now there's just no way because she's gone. So much of my perspective on communication has shifted because of that loss.

We often get hung up on the ins and outs of who should initiate and who should respond and how things come across, and we forget that it is a gift and an honor and a privilege to be able to communicate with one another at all. We treat one another with judgment and unspoken expectations rather than meeting one another right where we're at. We assume motives and intentions and jump to all kinds of conclusions.

And then we think to ourselves, *There's no way we can recover from this.*

• • • •

When Christ rises from the dead, an angel appears to the grieving women at his tomb and offers great news that He is alive. They are overcome with hope and joy and absolute shock. As they stand there, the angel gives them a very specific command:

"Don't be alarmed," he said. "You are looking for Jesus the Nazarene, who was crucified. He has risen! He is not here. See the place where they laid him. But go, tell his disciples and Peter, 'He is going ahead of you into Galilee. There you will see him, just as he told you.'" (Mark 16:6–7)

This specific mention of Peter is not a random coincidence. This is an extension of God's kindness. God is letting

Peter know that he is still loved and seen, and he especially needs to know that Jesus has risen and is coming to see *him*.

When the women share the news of Jesus's resurrection, the disciples don't believe them at first:

> But they did not believe the women, because their words seemed to them like nonsense. Peter, however, got up and ran to the tomb. Bending over, he saw the strips of linen lying by themselves, and he went away, wondering to himself what had happened. (Luke 24:11–12)

Peter is hoping that maybe, just maybe, it's true. In the most unexpected turn of events, he now finds himself watching and waiting for Jesus. He returns to his work as a fisherman, and one good morning, Jesus appears on the beach, providing them with breakfast. As they sit and talk, it would be easy enough for Jesus to sort of nod at Peter as if to imply, "We're cool. No worries, dude." Instead, He digs in.

Remember when Jesus saw Peter in Luke 22? That word for looking at him is the Greek word *emblepó*, which literally means "to look at with love or care or concern." Jesus wasn't angry; He was concerned. And there was no way He was going to leave that look and this situation up to Peter's imagination.

No, He chooses to very specifically communicate to Peter. And this communication actually offers reconciliation in a way that would not have happened had Jesus chosen to avoid an uncomfortable situation.

> When they had finished eating, Jesus said to Simon Peter, "Simon son of John, do you love me more than these?"
>
> "Yes, Lord," he said, "you know that I love you."
>
> Jesus said, "Feed my lambs."

> Again Jesus said, "Simon son of John, do you love me?"
> He answered, "Yes, Lord, you know that I love you."
> Jesus said, "Take care of my sheep."
> The third time he said to him, "Simon son of John, do you love me?"
> Peter was hurt because Jesus asked him the third time, "Do you love me?" He said, "Lord, you know all things; you know that I love you."
> Jesus said, "Feed my sheep." (John 21:15–17)

It seems that Jesus is being a little repetitive here, trying to drive home the fact that Peter denied Him three times and now Peter is telling Him he loves Him three times. But we have to remember that in Greek, there are multiple words for love. For example, there's *eros*, erotic love that is very physical and sexual and romantic. There's also *agape*, unconditional love that is the type of love God shows us. Don't forget about *phileo*, brotherly love (this is where the great city of Philadelphia gets its name).

Each time that Jesus asks him if he loves Him, Peter responds with brotherly love. He's trying to make things less intense because he feels a little called out at this moment. He's still trying to save face, ever so subtly, but Jesus can see right through it, so He leans in.

On the third ask, Peter slows down and lets himself take in the moment. He looks at Jesus, and finally, he responds that he loves Him in a true and unconditional way, using the word *agape*, which is much stronger than the love of a casual friend. He gets vulnerable for a moment and recommits himself to Jesus, and then Jesus responds by inviting him to continue doing the work that they have been doing for years now.

Jesus didn't have to go out of His way to have this conversation with Peter, and yet I believe it shows us the intentionality of our good God. He makes eye contact until Peter can receive His kindness and puts into words exactly what needs to be said so that there is *no question* about where Peter stands with Him.

Jesus saw the way Peter had promised faithfulness and then watched Peter deny Him and even locked eyes with him in the moment. There was no denying that Jesus knew the fullness of Peter's shame. And yet, He made sure Peter knew that he was still fully loved.

Peter didn't need to wonder if Jesus was holding anything against him as a result of the denial. Jesus was basically saying, "I know exactly what you did, and I want you to know that I love you and trust you. You are still invited into this work."

I once wrote an email to a friend, and she responded with time-sensitive information I skimmed over and quickly forgot. When she reached out again a month or so later to remind me, she restated that same information, and I was so surprised by it and acted like I'd never heard it.

Gently, she said, "I already told you this over a month ago so it shouldn't be a surprise."

I wanted to shift blame or pretend that I wasn't at fault, but the truth is, she was right. She had already given me that information, and what I needed to do was admit that I'd been hasty in my earlier reading and I was sorry to have blamed her for giving me "last-minute" info.

We have to stop holding on to our pride and use our words to pursue a willingness to be wrong and apologize for ways we haven't done right by others through our actions or words.

Communication isn't just about mending broken places or smoothing things over. It also makes sweet moments sweeter.

When my dear friends Jordan and Matt got married, I joyfully got a plane ticket and rented a car with other friends. We got dressed up, and the wedding day was a perfect spring afternoon—not too hot, not too cold. I saw the happy couple at the reception as usual and then prepared to go home the next day.

I had anticipated not having any one-on-one time with Jordan because it was her wedding weekend and there were about one million other things that she could be doing other than making time for me out of the hundreds of people involved in her big day. It was a joy and a delight to celebrate her and her now-husband Matt's marriage, and it was a fun reunion with some of our mutual friends.

A few hours before we had to fly home, my friends and I decided to grab food at a local restaurant. As we pulled up, we noticed a lot of Matt and Jordan's family pouring out of that very establishment and realized that there had been a brunch for the family that was just finishing up. We gave hugs to Jordan's mom and aunt and as we were walking in, Matt and Jordan appeared.

They were supposed to be on their way to North Carolina for a honeymoon, but as we got closer to the entrance of the building, we saw them unexpectedly walking toward us.

The new bride gave us a hug and said with all the confidence in the world, "We only have two hours to drive today, and all of our favorite people are here, so we thought that we would swing by and say hello for a little while. Why don't you go get some food, and we will join you!"

There was no use trying to convince her to go off to her honeymoon. She was determined to stay, and her husband was standing right beside her with the exact same priority: being with their community. You could not convince them that there was a better choice, and they did not want to leave anything unsaid so they spoke with their actions and joined us.

Weren't they tired? They had just thrown an incredible wedding party the night before, and I'm certain that after so many months of planning, they were exhausted. There were so many reasons they could have excused themselves and gone off to rest together, but that's not what they chose to do.

Jordan told us that she had already planned to take a nap on the road to North Carolina and that the next few days would be full of plenty of rest, but she wanted to take the time to check in with us and see how we were doing. This is what it looks like to communicate love.

It would have been so easy for them to stick around and say nothing about it, but instead, they chose to communicate that they wanted to be with us and they knew they had a road trip ahead of them and they were not regretting their choice. They communicated to us that they knew the cost, they'd counted it, and it was worth their investment to linger with us.

We ordered some food, and as we sat waiting, they walked over to us, sat down on the grass nearby, and played with my friend's nine-month-old son. We chatted like old friends do as if we were just visiting them for the weekend and all the pomp and circumstance had not just happened. For twenty minutes, we were just together, and it was good.

This simple twenty-minute detour in their day preached a way of life to me that I needed to remember. These friends delighted in people so much that they made it a priority to say, "Yes, I can be a little bit delayed for the sake of being right here, right now."

The willingness to be inconvenienced and the joyfulness of getting to be with another person is something that we do not live into enough. They so wonderfully used verbal communication ("Here are my intentions and I'm loving this decision to stick around") alongside taking action in a way that moved us all. They weren't just saying good things, they were doing good things.

If most communication is nonverbal, we have to make sure our words and actions line up.

Because of the way that Jordan and Matt live their lives, I have no doubt that I am loved by them, even during their big weekend. And what's amazing is that there are dozens of other people who also felt the exact same way that weekend because of the intentionality of the bride and groom to include others and to celebrate their marriage as a moment of community and not only as the love that they share between the two of them.

And isn't that the way it's supposed to be? Aren't we supposed to let each day be full of intentionality and communication with our friends and loved ones?

As a single woman, I genuinely feel that my relationship with Jordan has not changed or, if anything, that it has grown *stronger* since she began her relationship with her now-husband because, from the beginning, they both decided to value their communities and not become a silo.

Married people can become silos.

Single people can become silos.

None of us are immune to this tendency, but when we make the choice to let people know how we feel about them and show them the ways we value their presence, it radically transforms the way we receive love *and* the way we give it.

As a result of their interactions and because Jesus communicated how He felt, Peter knew that he was loved by Jesus, and it fueled him for the rest of his life, eventually leading him to martyrdom. This man who could not even admit he knew Jesus was now willing to give his entire life for Him.

Love sets us free to take risks, but we will never know we are loved if we don't hear it and experience it. We have the chance now to tell our people how we feel. We can reach out to our married friends and say, "I know it's been a while, but I'd love to reconnect." Or we can invite someone new and say, "I'm so excited to get to know you better!"

We are called the hands and feet of Christ because we represent Him to each other and if we're going to carry forth His legacy of intentional communication, we have to do that with forthrightness and kindness.

We have to speak words like we mean them and we have to proclaim love like it matters and we have to apologize and face hard truths. We have to roll up our sleeves and do the good work because we know that what is on the other side is reconciliation and growth and depth in relationship.

Leave nothing up to the imagination, y'all. Communicate exactly how you're feeling about your people out of a heart for building relationships—and mending them too.

six

Consistency

I struggled with consistency in friendships as a child, which led me to a place of feeling anxious about relationships altogether.

My very first best friend was a girl whose father was the pastor of the church I grew up in. We would spend Sunday afternoons together while her parents rested after the service, and we would run around together having all kinds of adventures, especially in the summer when school wasn't there to cramp our style. But during the spring when I was eight years old, El Niño swept through the West Coast and destroyed much of the California coastline, and she and her family moved all the way to the east side of Canada. I was heartbroken, but I still had a good friend down the street and another at school who were regular parts of my life. I love a backup plan.

My siblings had lifelong friends that they still have to this day, and I always wanted consistent friends so badly, so when my first best friend moved away, I was pretty determined to make sure that I had other friends to walk through life with. But then the friend who lived down the street moved to Idaho and the friend from school moved to Washington. I had one final hope in the form of a very quirky girl I could goof around with, but she ended up moving to Sacramento, six hours away.

I cannot tell you why it is that I didn't give up on friendship altogether. I know that my little heart was broken over and over again with each of these losses, but somehow I kept believing that friendship was possible. I'm fairly social by nature, so maybe I just had a resilience that was given to me by Jesus, but when I think back to that season between the ages of eight and eleven, I can see my ache for consistency.

I think it's funny that God has made us to desire relationships that are nurtured by consistency when the world that we live in is fairly inconsistent. The only constant is change, right?

Perhaps this is the juxtaposition of our faith in relationship to the lived experience of the short time we have here on this side of eternity. We were made for more than fits and starts. We were made for relationships that do not break or move or walk away when conflict arises. No, we were made for relationships that stay and take a seat and kick off their shoes and say things like, "I have nowhere else to be. Take your time."

Sometimes I wonder if my childhood of inconsistent friendships is the thing that prepared me best for singleness. So often we become close to someone and then they meet The One and their affections can shift. It is not a bad thing for somebody to love their spouse, but it definitely can make things feel tricky when we are the ones always seemingly being left behind. To be fair, sometimes we truly *are* left behind as someone begins a new chapter of their life. It is a complicated thing to lose a friendship to marriage because on the one hand, we're very happy that they have found someone they can partner with for the rest of their lives, but on the other hand, we have to acknowledge the reality that we lose out on what our friendship with them was like up until that point. Sometimes, love can be costly—not only for the people exchanging rings.

I believe that there is a way forward into friendship with our friends who are married, but we also need to address the elephants in the room, because they're adding up and we're running out of space and it's getting harder and harder to ignore some of these painful realities of being a single person.

So much of the pain in our relationships is due to the fact that we aren't coming to them authentically, but strategically. For a long time, we've been trained to think about relationships as transactional. We wonder, *What am I getting from this?*

Here's what I mean by that: Sometimes, in our own short-sightedness, we forget that friendship is about the deep need we have for connection and communion. We forget that it is something that creates good things in us and isn't just there to serve us. As humans, we are constant objectifiers and optimizers, and sometimes that trickles into our relationships as well. There's nothing wrong with streamlining our grocery lists or routes for errands, but we can't optimize our friendships.

While it seems like a positive thing to want to make "better" relationships by choosing "better" quality people, we're actually keeping score and hurting ourselves and others because we're trying to form other people in our own image instead of remembering that we are created beings who are being conformed only to the image of Jesus. He is where we find our identity. He is the one we are trying to be like.

Because the fact of the matter is that if we try to forge relationships to be what we expect them to be based on our preferences and needs, we're going to be let down. What I wanted in a friend in my twenties is different from what I'm hoping for now in my thirties, and I'm so glad that instead of trying to form friendships based on a list of qualities I thought I wanted, I asked Jesus to send the right friends into my life. He always knows best, and I'm always changing my mind anyway.

Sometimes, we consider potential friendships with others but we don't see the ways *we* might change or grow over time. We place expectations on them to fulfill *our* needs in the moment. Sometimes we aren't building friendships based on companionship or care, but on trying to check boxes of what we think we want in a friend. This is dangerous territory to stumble into.

First, it's going down a pathway of looking to people for our satisfaction, and while people can certainly meet practical needs or relational needs, they cannot be the ultimate source of satisfaction in our souls. Inevitably, someone's going to let someone down and we'll be back at square one. Second, when we see people as friends who can fill needs, we see them as having purpose only in relation to us. We see them as happiness makers and not complex humans who we are able to walk alongside and enjoy and delight in and support. If we choose our friends based on who makes us feel the best or offers us the most stability and support, we are actually no better than the popular kids who create social hierarchies.

Frankly, I saw that enough when I was a teenager and now that my brain is fully developed, I'm not here for that nonsense.

It's understandable that we want to be friends with people we enjoy and who we have a lot of shared interests with, and that can certainly be a great starting point. But when that becomes the primary way we measure our friendships, we can become solely focused on our own happiness and satisfaction, so when things get complicated, it can be easier to choose to end a friendship than work through the conflict and grow in connection with one another. Thus, our friendships can fall apart without a chance to grow. When we choose to be fair-weather about our friendships instead of sticking through when things get messy, we end up constantly riding the roller coaster of making friends, experiencing conflict, and then abandoning ship. Consistency means being present in those messy moments and walking through them—together.

If we're going to build friendships that can survive the intensity of the storms of life, we're going to have to learn to be more stalwart. As a New Englander, that's one of my favorite words. It has to do with shipbuilding. An old sailing vessel is considered stalwart if it can withstand heavy amounts of pressure without leaking. If a ship is well-built, it is stalwart. If a ship lasts for years and years, it is stalwart. If a ship can endure a great storm, it is stalwart.

If we want to be consistent friends, we have to build our friendships in a hearty way. The presence of stalwart character is what will make all the difference in staying put.

Down the road from me is a town called Essex that carries a long history of shipbuilding. Many towns around here carry a history of unique trades, but Essex has always caught my attention because of its role in maritime history. I got my first lesson on this history when I became friends with the owner of an antique store one fateful afternoon.

I'm writing this in the office of that antique store as I look out over the marsh. My friend Cathy is up at the register as usual, running things and making sure that this business continues to survive the insane downturn that has plagued the antique industry for the last few years. At its height, there were dozens of antique stores lining the causeway of this small town. Now there are just a handful left, but this particular one has a whole lot of character mostly because of the characters inside.

In the late fall of 2020, I walked into the store to look for a Christmas tree topper, and an older man in red suspenders was sitting in the window, greeting people as they came and went. His name was Ed, and he asked me what I was looking for. I told him I was willing to settle for just about anything as long as it could go on a tree. After grabbing a handful of small items, I worked my way to the cash register with the few dollars I had. There were no tree toppers, but that didn't stop Ed from offering me his nautical New Englander advice: Put a buoy on top of your tree. He got up, walked out the front door, and shuffled down the brick stairs and around the corner to the driveway where there were a bunch of lobster buoys sitting in a giant pile.

I sifted through them and found one that had teal, deep orange, and white stripes and I took it home with me. I set up my tree (complete with buoy) and enjoyed my holidays, and when some friends came to visit, I took them back to the antique store because I had so enjoyed the conversation I had with Ed.

During our initial conversations, he asked me what I did and because I didn't have a job at that time, I told him I was a writer. No matter what happens in my vocation, I can always claim that, right? As I wandered around the store with my friends, he remembered me and shuffled over to where I was. In a mysterious and very endearing way, he motioned for me to come with him to his back office because he said he needed to discuss something with me. He was very serious and intentional, but it had an undertone of mischief, which I would later learn was his way.

I walked into his back office, which had wood-paneled walls covered in photos of ships and maritime-themed art, and took a seat in the green chair beside his desk. I waited, unsure of what was coming next from this very new friend.

Ed looked at me with his blue eyes and said, "I need to tell you something that you might not believe even if I told you, but then again, maybe you would."

My eyebrows raised in surprise. He had my attention, and he knew it.

He proceeded to tell me that many different things had happened to him over the years and he wanted someone to tell them to who would write them down. I agreed to meet with him every Thursday for an hour or two or three and hear what he had to share. Very quickly, I realized that this wasn't about note-taking or even about writing a book of Ed's stories; it was about an older man who was looking for friendship and a young woman who had a lot of time on her hands and was willing to join him on that journey. Ed was a man who had spent much of his life on the water in ships and boats, and his experience made for endless hours of stories and rants and opinions no one asked for but that needed to be stated nonetheless.

Ed was sharp as a tack and clever as all get-out, and he often talked about how he never wanted to be like those older people who ride around in buses and go on tours. When the town hosted pancake breakfasts for older adults, he complained that there were too many old people there. He wanted to be active and alive and curious and adventuresome all the way to the very end.

Two things he gave me a love for were maritime history and old New England architecture. The antique store itself is in a building that was erected in the 1700s, and when you go into the basement or other parts of the house where you can see exposed beams, you will notice that there are no nails because the entire frame was built without any. The builders knew how to make a home that was so well-built it could withstand nearly anything.

With harsh winters and unforgiving storms, the Essex community has built a whole legacy of going out onto the waters. Gloucester, which is just next door, boasts the oldest seaport in America, and while that is impressive, it also means that over the course of the last few hundred years, thousands of sailors have gone out and not returned. The residents here understand that the sea is wild and dangerous but also a part of life that allows this community to exist, so they continue to set sail.

The people who framed the antique store with pieces of wood that were wedged together and could not be moved are the same ones who framed ships and built them like their lives depended on them, because they did. You would not go out on a ship that was not stalwart. And making sure that a ship was seaworthy was absolutely vital to the success of the work you were given to do.

Ed did not enter a friendship with me in a half-hearted way. He was sharp and animated, always telling me the latest town *chisme*, always filling me in on what was going on. One visit turned into countless visits on endless Thursdays. Our consistency was present for years, which, to a gal who struggled early on to keep friendships, was most unexpected and came surprisingly naturally.

As we think about consistency in friendships as single people, let's consider some practical ways we can do that for one another. I think the best place to start is to keep coming back, even when it feels like there's not a lot of progress.

I struggled at times to show up for Ed. I made stupid excuses to myself about why I wasn't sure I had time to get to the antique store. In the winter I had an especially hard time bundling up to make my way there. But somehow I managed to keep those excuses to myself and forced myself to put on a coat and drive the fifteen minutes out to Essex.

Ed was diagnosed with Parkinson's long before we met and as he got older he needed more help with mobility, so his doctors recommended that he get some kind of a cane. Ever convinced he was not an old person, he suggested that both of us get walking sticks, as if I needed the stability as much as he did. I gently agreed and our walking sticks are still in my car.

Ed's doctor told him that a good way to keep mobility as he got older was to walk a mile a day. He swore to me that he was doing it, but Cathy and I were sure he was fudging the numbers a bit. We knew this because he and I would go on short walks to the harbor, and he always had to stop to lean on the railing of the causeway bridge.

Conveniently, he had so many fun facts that he had to pause and share one every hundred feet or so.

I saw he was declining but we walked anyway. The slow shuffle of Ed's gait felt maddening at times because I was both wanting to move faster and was also very worried that he was going to fall over.

When I got a new job that was going to remove my flexibility, I thought about meeting with Ed less. Or maybe I'd tell him that I just couldn't hang out so much. But still, something in me whispered, "Wait. Hold on a moment. See what happens when you stay consistent."

Consistency is like adding to a bank account. One deposit at a time, you store up more than you realize. Each yes and each conversation and each meal turns out to be an investment into friendship in the richest ways.

You cannot say that you have a close friend if you're not consistently showing up. It could be a text or a trip to the grocery store or a movie night or grabbing dinner before class. Consistency doesn't need to be constant to be significant. But it does mean showing up over and over again.

Ed invited me to a livestream of his favorite opera, *La traviata*, and we dressed up to go to a local theater to watch it. He invited me to tea at Dunkin' Donuts where he complained that the chairs were flimsy and the air conditioner was on. I came to his birthday dinner where I gave him a book from my childhood called *I Spy* because his antique store reminded me of the pages of the search-and-find-style book.

We walked along the marsh, we shared lunch, we took his first-ever selfie, and he made comments about how women should wear dresses more often. His old-school outlook and my willingness to sit and chat worked out well, and one day, I realized that we were really becoming friends. We were being consistent. We were putting in the effort and that consistency was braiding our lives together.

And when storms came, we were able to ride them out together. Ed lost his wife and his sister, and we shuffled across the street to a seafood restaurant. I ordered us french fries, and he told me what he'd been carrying as he grieved. I shared with him about a beloved friend struggling with addiction, and he offered wisdom on how to care well. He had walked many roads before that were new terrain for me.

We weren't just cruising along. Sometimes it felt like we were taking on water, and I didn't know what it would look like to stay afloat. It just sort of blurred together, the good and the hard. But like a seam that perfectly aligns between two pieces of wood, we were watertight.

Consistency is one small commitment at a time. It arrives like a piece of mail that surprises and delights, and then each time you open the mailbox and find another piece, you come to expect the joy it provides. If you had told me that my friendship with Ed was going to take up so many regular hours and days right from the start, I would have said I didn't know if I could commit to that. But instead, we worked away at something lovely, the way Ed worked away at the salvaged antiques in his workshop that he tightened and adjusted and gave new life to.

What I am here for is building relationships that allow us to weather the storms that we face as single people and even along other routes if we end up with a spouse one day. Because here is the thing: The consistency of having a partner is great, but single people are entitled to regularity and consistency too. There is nothing about our humanity that changes when we get married. It's not like we become completely different people. When you move to a new town or start a new job or just change hair products, you have the same pet peeves and the same personality quirks and you're dealing with the same history and life experience.

See, the choices you make and the habits you form right now are going to influence who you are and how you live years down the road. If you make people a priority and show up in and out of season, at some point they're just part of your life, and you don't have to make appointments or small talk anymore. No, one day, your lives are just shared—and it doesn't matter if you're coming from different perspectives.

Consistency is like muscle memory. Repeated motions have a way of sticking with us. But also? Our muscles are conditioned by the impact that they experience and the trauma that they endure. Like relearning to walk after having a broken leg, it's hard to trust that something that was suddenly so unstable could ever be stable again. All the consistency in the world can be challenged by a bad fall or an accident. So it can't be as simple as a formula, as much as I wish that it was.

I used to tell people I hated the idea of a best friend because it was too exclusive. The truth was that I was so afraid of calling anyone the best because it might not work out. After all, it hadn't worked out a whole lot of times before. My fear of what could happen eclipsed my desire to pursue close friendships.

Has this ever happened to you? Has a past pain marked you in a way that makes you no longer want to pursue good things?

First of all, I am so sorry that you went into something hoping for a soft place to land and were met with something completely unexpected and grief-laden. But can I tell you something? I promise you that you were made to be in consistent community and friendship that does not fade. And that's coming from the woman who used to say goodbye over and over again. I promise you that Jesus is in the midst of your relational heartache and that taking the risk of consistency is well worth it, even when things start to unravel.

Ed and I have not been on a walk with those walking sticks in over nine months because Parkinson's and age have caught up with him. He doesn't know where he is most of the time, and when I visit him at the memory care facility he's been living in for several months, he does not know who I am. He does not know that we sat for hours and talked about everything under the sun. He does not know that we've walked along the causeway countless times. He does not know about sitting on a bench and talking about hopes and dreams while looking out over the Great Marsh where the ships used to sail out to the Atlantic.

But I remember everything and I cannot get our friendship out of my head because we were so consistent for so long and what we built was seaworthy.

There is very little that Ed can give me in practical ways. He used to help me fix furniture I found on the side of the road or offer advice that I did not ask for about dating, and he used to pay when we got tea and a bagel at Dunkin' Donuts. But these days? I cannot measure our friendship if I tried. I cannot quantify the benefits of friendship with someone fifty years older in a way that is a measurable outcome or perceived profit.

Because that's not how friendship works. Friendship isn't fueled by consumption; it's fueled by consistency.

All we can do is show up every day and see what it turns into, asking Jesus to meet us in the places we don't understand. Sometimes friendships come and go and that's okay. And sometimes, long after a person has gone in some way or another, the friendship stays. But we will never know if we don't show up and build something stalwart together. We will never know if we think about only what people can do for us or how we can benefit in some way that gets us ahead.

When I drive through Essex, I remember that making friends is like building a good ship. It takes consistency and many hands and there are splinters involved, but when you make it out into the open ocean, it will withstand more than you thought possible.

seven

Closeness

Evening walks in early September are the perfect result of warm afternoons that give way to cool breezes as the sun sets. I can wear my favorite combination of shorts and running shoes and a sweatshirt that may or may not be needed. I cross over to the local park and walk along sidewalks that carry me through the woods and into a community garden. Before I know it, I'm in the next town over, which isn't saying much around these parts where town boundaries are like scribbles that overlap constantly.

The air smells sweet and the crickets are out and when I get back to my apartment, I pull a frozen meal from Trader Joe's out. While it heats up, I open a drink and kick off my shoes and take a seat by the open window. In a matter of moments, I'll be under a soft blanket, planning the week ahead. I'll consider what social commitments I have and what meetings might be on the horizon, send out a few texts, and maybe watch some reruns of early episodes of *Survivor*.

As the night fully falls, I watch people vote each other off the island and make jokes to myself about how amazing the early 2000s were when it comes to reality television. Slowly I'll feel the wear-down from a weekend that was a bit fuller than I thought it'd be, and I'll change into my pajamas and head to the bathroom for the usual face washing and tooth-brushing. And then? I'll open the medicine cabinet and pull out my retainer.

I got it when I was seventeen years old and, doing the math right now, I do wonder if I should get it replaced. All I know is that it has polka dots and when my orthodontist gave me specific instructions to wear it every night, I took him seriously. Here I am, all these years later, wearing the retainer almost every single night as I crawl into bed.

Very few people have seen me on a night like this one. There's no dinner party or movie night or planned hangout—it's just me by myself. I've had evenings like this countless times, and it feels so familiar, but no one is close enough to me to see this on a regular basis. Most of the time I don't "feel" my singleness, but on quiet nights like this, I feel a distance between me and the world around me that makes me want to add another blanket and sink a little deeper into the couch.

I'm not alone in feeling a lack of proximity in my life. When I've asked single friends in real life and online about what they're lacking most, they respond with a resounding cry of "I need physical touch."

Any time I ask these kinds of questions, I always expect people to answer with thoughts on needing community or financial stability, and while a few of those answers trickle in, the one I see that hits me right in the gut is when people say they just want a hug.

I grew up in an era of Christianity in which we were taught to fear intimacy in many different ways because, in most conversations, intimacy was equated to sexual intimacy. The message we were given about sexual purity was well-intentioned, but I think it may have reinforced the idea that if we feel a desire to be close in any way with an individual, we should probably question it or fight against it. I used to believe that having a need for closeness showed some sort of defect on my part, and as a result, I was relationally and emotionally stunted in some ways. I didn't believe that showing emotion was appropriate, so only a handful of people ever saw me cry until I was in college. I didn't believe that sharing personal information was wise, so some of the more traumatic and challenging parts of my story were only known by about three people until I was in my twenties.

Yes, we want to be wise about oversharing, but many of us overcorrect into distancing ourselves from *any* kind of vulnerability. My generation in the church was very good at listening when others told us what *not* to do, but at times that left us wondering what *to* do with the very natural impulses we have for closeness.

I would read Scripture for the rules and regulations of the game of life that I was playing. I looked for morality and a set of beliefs that would guide me as I grew in my faith. But it wasn't until much later that I started reading Scripture to also understand the complexities of the human condition. I was always only looking for the lesson or the three-point takeaway, not realizing that we can learn a whole lot from Jesus by observing the *way* that He interacted with others and not only by skipping to the words that He spoke. Don't get me wrong; His teachings are absolutely essential, but like any good mentor or teacher, we also love them for how they exist and not only what they say during a lesson. The most influential mentors and leaders in my life have spoken truth but have also lived it out and had a way about them that was compelling. It was ministry to my heart to simply be in close proximity to them.

John was a disciple and writer of the New Testament and he referred to himself as "the disciple whom Jesus loved" (John 13:23). He did not show up to the party with all of the education or clout or accolades, but he knew full well that he was deeply loved by Jesus. I find this incredibly comforting, because if Jesus only loved the people who were impressive, it would set the bar entirely too high for us, and we wouldn't even bother trying to reach it.

Jesus had this incredible way about Him where He cherished whoever was in front of Him and did not look at how impressive their social standing was. He proclaimed to them with His inviting nature, "Get over here, friend."

Throughout the narrative of John's Gospel, we see Jesus perform miracles and invest in the disciples and be a light in the very dark world. Toward the end of the book, there is a particularly poignant scene in which Jesus is sharing a Passover meal with His disciples. He is the only one who understands that this will be their last opportunity to be gathered before the intensity of His trial and crucifixion, underscoring the future interactions they're going to have. Passover is a holiday in which an extravagant meal is eaten, and this is one of the traditions of their Jewish heritage, so this meal is not only celebratory but familiar. Familiar settings allow for a more relaxed experience, and we see that played out in the fact that several times in this story, John mentions that he was resting on Jesus.

John is not suggesting that he was resting near Jesus or next to Jesus, but that he was actually leaning on Him. It's the kind of closeness that indicates true trust and letting your guard down. Exhaling in peace and settling in.

Some translations say that he was resting on the breast of Jesus. This image is incredibly tender and intimate and is meant to show us the sort of closeness and trust that Jesus had with His disciples. This interaction between Him and John is not sterile and distanced and strictly professional; it is *close*.

One could argue that it's just a funny turn of phrase, that John would not have been so vulnerable, but he mentions it multiple times, which authors tend to do to paint a specific picture with accuracy. This meal is not just a gathering of random people or something that is Instagram-worthy and soon to be forgotten in their memory. No, John wrote this after the crucifixion, knowing full well what was about to take place, and yet he retold the story with attention to the relational details because he wanted us to understand that Jesus loved His disciples. Throughout this book, the word *love* is used over and over again until it becomes a theme and anthem. John is not just presenting us with facts and information; he is trying to relay to us that Christ did these things because He cared deeply, and His presence was cherished. In short: His ministry was one of proximity.

Sometimes, after we lose someone that we love, we look back to moments of connection with fondness. John wrote this book after Jesus had already ascended and was no longer physically present, and I wonder if perhaps he wrote those words to also remind himself that the friendship they shared was real and good. It was not only that of a mentor and a mentee but of brothers. They were family.

So often, we believe that church is a place where we are meant to be put together and not to ask for too much. We believe that the church is a place that is filtered, and we forget that the church was born out of a faith that focuses on a Savior who lets people draw close. He did not shy away from the woman at the well who was a social pariah, and He interacted with her in a way that many others wouldn't have. He invited children to come to Him and embraced them and delighted in them. He let His friend rest his head on His shoulder as they dined, knowing that everything was about to go to hell for a while.

Jesus was not measured with His closeness because He was not afraid of drawing near. In fact, when His presence was predicted in Scripture, He was given the name Emmanuel, which literally means "God with us." If we're out here wondering why it is that we are aching to be close to other human beings, we do not need to look any further than the fact that our Creator was named for proximity. And if we were made in His image, it is a good and beautiful thing that we desire closeness—because He Himself *is* closeness.

When we long for close connection and comfort and proximity, our souls are crying out for Jesus.

It is wild to me that this image of Jesus is not the one we often lead with. We like to tell people about His miracles and His power, and while those things are integral to who He is, I don't know if those things make us want to turn and face Him, to make eye contact and bring Him our aches and joys alike. Sometimes, we forget about what theologians call the hypostatic union.

The hypostatic union is a theological term that means that Jesus is fully God and fully man. He is not 50/50, He is not a little more one than the other. No, He is completely divine and completely human, 100 percent and 100 percent.

So often, we read about His extraordinary acts, and I think we forget about the human part. We forget about the part that is intensely relatable, and we are so focused on His otherness (also called *holiness*) that we take a few steps back, which is funny because He is inviting us to take a few steps forward. In an age of Greek mythology and Roman gods, there was no shortage of deities who were too great to condescend to humankind, let alone die for them.

Zeus would never.

Friend, did you know that you have a Savior who comes to you? Did you know that you have a Savior who desires to be near you? Did you know that you have a Savior who could have stayed very far away but He intentionally chose to show up in the middle of the mess and the mire and the masterpiece that He had created so that we might be set free?

If you are believing in your heart of hearts that as a single person you are not wired for or allowed closeness, then I need to tell you right now that you are believing something that is not true.

Yes, you may not experience the same physical intimacy that someone who is married does, but that does not mean that you can't have closeness at all. No, you have longings to draw near to others that Christ put there on purpose. All of the desires of our hearts point ultimately to satisfaction in Jesus. He does not leave us hanging, and He has not forgotten about those who do not have a spouse. The experience of genuine friendship and close connection is not only for the married or dating among us.

Our need to be close to others is just as valid as anyone else's. Our longing to sit shoulder to shoulder on the couch with someone we care about, even in a totally platonic way, is good and is even what our bodies were meant to experience.

The Family Institute at Northwestern University finds that "physical contact of a non-sexual nature—the hugs and squeezes, the handholding, the random touches—can be an effective pathway for maintaining intimacy."[1]

We will build better relationships if we can be physically present with others. You know how it feels when someone makes eye contact with you or asks you to sit with them at a meal. Gathering and communing is vital to the work of connecting to others in a close way.

After all, we are not souls floating in space. No, we are bodies that God has created for a myriad of experiences, and we get to be close to others as a way of building intimacy.

While this can feel complex as a single person, we know that God has made our bodies good. In her book *Real Sex*, Lauren Winner writes, "Bodies are who we are and where we live; they are not just things that God created us with, but means of knowing Him and abiding with Him."[2]

The next part of this is where we have to get a little bit brave. Because we sometimes have to not only acknowledge what we want, but we also have to be willing to ask others for it. For example, when I walk into a room, I can greet a dear friend from a few feet away, or I can walk up and say, "Hey, I haven't been hugged in like three days. Can I just have a hug?" Does it feel childish? Yup. Do I feel frustrated that I even need to ask and wish that I didn't? You bet. But do I also receive a hug, and does that friend know that in the future it might be a good idea to give me one? Absolutely.

We all have these things that we wish we had, and we don't know how to ask for them. While writing this book, I came down with mono. I had gone to a writing retreat with about thirty friends, and we were all sharing drinks and chips and guac and it was wonderful, but someone there was carrying mono. I had never gotten it before, so it hit me hard about six weeks later. When I got the diagnosis, I was two months away from finishing this book's manuscript, and I started to spiral because I was being told by doctors that I would be struggling with absolute exhaustion and flu-like symptoms for the next few months. My dream of sitting and writing on my own strength went out the window because I had no more strength left and about thirty thousand words to go.

As I sat and tried to figure out my next steps, I knew I needed help. I wanted my friends to just intuit how much I was going to need support. Every night when I got home from work, the idea of having to come up with dinner and prepare it felt so overwhelming that I would lie on the couch, paralyzed.

One day, my friend Rachel showed up at my house and helped me organize one of those meal train things where you can schedule meals for someone who's recently had a surgery or a baby or a major loss. It felt immensely vulnerable because I am a grown woman, and on the outside, I appeared to be okay, but I also knew that receiving help was going to be a game changer. A few days later, my friend Becky sent me a text asking how she could support me with my recovery, and I told her that I needed to ask for help but I didn't want to.

"You would happily jump on a meal train for your people, am I right?" she asked.

"Yes, but it feels so extra for me to ask," I confessed.

"You would gladly pitch in if one of your friends needed help. Jesus is with you and He loves you and all of your extra needs and wants you to ask for whatever you need."

She wasn't wrong. And as a result of reaching out to her and a few others, I was able to have a weekly meal that turned into three or four leftover meals for the following few weeks as I continued to write and finish this book. The fact that I did not need to desperately run to the grocery store on a Sunday night during those days changed the way I experienced rest and healing. Sometimes being willing to step out into the awkwardness allows us to get what we need.

Take a moment and consider how you're doing right now. Slow your breathing and try to set down the things you have in your mind for a moment. What do you want? What do you need? Do you need a hug? Do you need to share a meal with someone? Do you need to just have someone you can talk to on the phone? Then, consider asking friends to help you with these needs. Here's what that could look like:

"Hey, friend, I'm going through a season in which I'm feeling kind of lonely, and I'm wondering if we could go on a walk someday this week and just have a conversation about what's going on in our lives. There's nothing major I need to discuss; I just want some connection with a friend."

Or, "This is going to sound a little silly, but I don't think I have had a hug consistently for the last few weeks, and I'm wondering if I could swing by your apartment for a hug and a hello maybe once a week for the next couple weeks?

Sometimes, being single can be really hard because there's no one when I need a quick hug on a whim."

I think that most of the time, we don't voice these needs, and we're walking around in want, feeling all the more isolated because we're not even talking to other single friends about these aches. But I can tell you: We really want these things. My DMs are full of single friends who are wanting the same things and are not sure how to talk about it.

So let me go first and say, I want closeness! I want a hug and to share a meal with a friend and then sit side by side and laugh together at a favorite TV show. I want to sit and read while someone else sits and reads by me and to just not be alone.

It seems that we're missing out on these confessions, and I have been consistently surprised by how opening up to listen about the actual state of things has cultivated a sense of closeness in my friendships and has also allowed me to get the closeness that God has given me a desire for. While some friends might not be particularly touchy, they might be into taking walks or chatting on the phone or even just receiving your prayer requests and bringing them to Jesus.

Each person is wired a little bit differently, and when we can uniquely show up for individual friends, we are able to connect in genuine ways that are meaningful for everyone involved. Because here's the thing: Our non-single friends have needs as well. Many young moms believe that they are failing constantly and need the affirmation that they're doing a good job. Those who are in intense seasons of financial struggle or job loss may be feeling like they don't want to share too much or in a way that feels too exposing for their partner. But being able to talk about these things openly and without judgment might be exactly what they need.

The need for closeness that we feel so acutely is felt by everyone and is not satisfied only in our relationship status. The more that I throw out my needs to others and they receive them and help meet them, ultimately pointing me back to Jesus for my deepest satisfaction, the more I realize what a joy it is to do the same for them.

Sometimes, closeness can be trusting someone with our stories or inviting them into our messy homes when we're under the weather and desperately needing some support. Because at the end of the day, closeness is what we were designed for and what we want to receive in more ways than just through physical touch. We are not only comforted with hugs but also with kindness and words and prepared meals and about a thousand other points of close connection that you can only make by drawing near.

I know plenty of people who do not respond well to physical touch, but they cannot get enough encouraging notes. Others love getting help with an organization project or for someone to offer to help them clean out their car. At this point in time, pretty much everyone is aware of Gary Chapman's *The 5 Love Languages*.³ It's a wildly popular bestselling book, and the whole premise is that we all receive love in different ways, and we need to learn how to offer love in the way that people best feel cared for. One friend does not like physical touch, so a hug is not going to mean a ton to her, but she does appreciate an act of service, and so when I go to visit and I help her do the dishes, that speaks volumes. Another friend lights up when she receives a letter expressing appreciation or offering encouragement. Still another friend loves physical touch and greets those she cares for with a big, welcoming hug. Every person that I am close to has a language that allows them to feel loved, but beyond that, learning how they receive love allows us to actually become closer and to cultivate continued closeness.

I know that being single can often feel more like a curse than a gift, and I'm not here to tell you that being single is some sort of magic thing we need to be thankful for all the time. We've heard that enough, and I think it's pretty trite. But I also believe that being single allows us to be sensitive to the needs we have as humans when we do not have a partner helping fill in some of the gaps. We are extra sensitive to the emotions others feel, and it allows us to be sensitive to their needs. It helps us to be better friends when we can pull someone close and say, "Yes, same."

Singleness allows me to take rich joy in friendships that are entirely platonic. We often start a relationship with someone who is the opposite sex and wonder, even for just a moment, if maybe they're a potential partner. But over time, I have found that this mindset is a wrong first step in friendship because we need to see others as beloved friends before we see them as potential partners.

If I'm watching guys walk into a coffee shop and my first move is to check for wedding rings or fish around to find out relationship statuses, it's the wrong posture. Instead, I want to cultivate a genuine and platonic connection with brothers and sisters in Christ, seeing them as companions before I jump to anything else.

Because friendships are the vast majority of our relationships! And we need to learn how to build healthy nonsexual intimacy with those around us. How to lean on one another with vulnerability like John leaned on Jesus.

We know what it is to be lonely, and we know what it is to have no one to turn to. We know what it's like to have great news and no one to celebrate with. And we know that it can be hard to go first and say, "Wow, that sounds lonely. How can I help?" But each time we draw near to one another and ask good questions and build deeper friendships, we're better off.

We know what it is to feel a lack of closeness, and it allows us to draw near to those around us in a way that pulls us all toward the heart of Jesus. Collectively, we move in until we are resting on His breast, feeling the rise and fall as His lungs expand, and it steadies us, drawing us closer and closer until our breathing slows and we know deep down that we belong right here, beside Jesus.

eight

Courage

In college, I majored in electronic media, a fancy term for film, radio, and television. One afternoon after class, a professor of mine asked me to stay back so he could talk to me about something. One by one, students left the classroom until he and I were standing there, and I was certain that he wanted to talk about my grade because I was an average student at best, always more willing to have adventures with my dorm mates than put in extra time studying. But instead of lecturing me about my most recent paper or assignment, he asked if I had plans over spring break and told me that they needed a photographer and videographer for a trip that he and his colleague were leading to the Holy Land. This professor happened to be one of the leading experts on Israel and Bible history, so he went several times every year to teach and guide.

I told him that I didn't even have a passport, but I absolutely wanted to go so I would see what I could do to make it happen. I went to the embassy—which conveniently was located only a few blocks away because I went to college in downtown Chicago—and they were able to expedite it so I received my passport just a few days later. Without much of a second thought, I packed my bags and got on a plane to New York, which then connected me to a flight to Tel Aviv.

It was a whirlwind trip: once-in-a-lifetime sort of stuff. One day I was sitting in my dorm, and the next I was with buses full of strangers who were eager to learn about Jesus and the Bible and walk in the places that we read about. We stood on the Mount of Beatitudes and we walked the alleyways through marketplaces and we pressed our written prayers into the Western Wall. I took photos and videos and captured the sights and sounds and light and food and didn't feel alone at all because I was surrounded by other participants of the tour. I'm a quick friend-maker, so I felt that I had my people with me, to some degree.

Until one very jet-lagged morning.

My sleep had been off because I was on the other side of the world, and whatever strange circadian rhythm happened to be flowing through my body that day woke me up just before the sun rose over the Dead Sea. I was staying in a hotel room by myself with a little balcony that overlooked the water, and I knew that if I fell asleep again, I might not wake up in time to get the bus. So I grabbed my journal and my Bible, and I stepped out onto the warm tile, sat down, and took in the view.

Even now, fifteen years later, I can feel the surprising warmth of the sun so early in the morning on my skin. I can see the haze of the desert surrounding the Dead Sea, and I can feel how easy it is to breathe at the lowest point on

Earth. The elevation made me feel like a superhero and I ran the best 5K of my life on the treadmill at the hotel.

As the sky lit up gold and the quietness of the surrounding area kept things at peace, I was suddenly struck with a very unexpected feeling: loneliness. I wanted to turn to someone and ask what they thought of the view. I wanted to share this moment that was so sacred and simple and good with another person, but there was no one there. Even in a group of two hundred, there was a buddy system, and I didn't have a buddy. I remember so acutely feeling like I was by myself, and then came a new wave of sadness as I realized that this memory would only be in my head.

Suddenly, I felt like I needed something unexpected: courage. Not courage to face something actively scary, but courage to experience something by myself. When you're single, sadness holds hands with courage.

Courage to make reservations and stay in a hotel room alone and see a new city by myself. Courage to figure out taxes or buy a new couch or begin a new job by myself. It doesn't matter how exciting transition or growth can be. The fact of the matter is that sadness is still in the room, lingering just close enough to be on the outskirts of the action. Close enough to be felt, even if not obviously seen.

Courage would not be necessary if we were not troubled. The weight of our ache feels light in some moments, and it feels overpowering in others. This leaves us having to figure out how on earth we're going to keep going, often believing we need to get rid of the sadness in order to keep moving forward. But you know what? Sadness on this side of heaven will not go away, so we have to walk alongside it and have the courage to do so.

In that moment, as I looked out over the sparkling water, I felt courage and sadness together. Because I knew that if one day I ended up meeting a man with whom I'd share my life, I could only describe to him what I saw. He would never know what it was like to be right there, right then. And even if we went back to that same hotel overlooking the salty sea and the crystalline shorelines, there would probably be new buildings and different conditions, and it would not be just as I remembered.

Up to that point, I had been journaling pretty regularly, trying to capture every last detail of this trip, but shortly after my moment on the balcony, I stopped. I wish I hadn't. I think I was feeling so overcome with so many new things and feelings and not knowing quite how to document them, so I decided not to document them in words at all.

It's very rare that you know the gravity of an experience while you're living it. But something was marked in my brain on that balcony, and that feeling of longing for another person who may or may not exist would rise to the surface a few other times.

It came back one fall when I was in Scotland visiting friends and I was walking to the old course at St. Andrews. It's historically considered the first official golf course, and this was a once-in-a-lifetime moment for me as an avid golfer. I was in the birthplace of the greatest game ever played. The weather was dreary but not rainy, I was wearing my L.L.Bean boots and a fleece vest and my favorite oxford shirt, and the vibe was immaculate.

Another time, I sat in my tiny dorm room of that big brick house in seminary and had just received my cap and gown for my master's. A day or two later, I put on a favorite dress and my black heels from high school—the only ones I owned until about 2024—and as I stood next to my little twin bed and made sure I wasn't missing anything, I had the distinct feeling that I was missing *someone*. Because I knew that from that moment on, I would have graduated from seminary, and whoever I ended up with one day, if I did end up with someone one day, would not have known me before I walked across that stage.

I'm not someone who regularly imagined myself getting married and I would consider myself to be fairly content in my singleness most of the time, but somewhere, buried in some old notebooks, are random pages where I used to write letters when the moment of not sharing an experience was too overwhelming. I told this imaginary person what had happened and why I wanted them to be there and what would have happened if they had been there, and I always would end the notes wishing them well and acknowledging that they may or may not exist. Because, whether or not I get married, the feeling of longing for a partner is just as real and just as valid.

That's the thing about wanting—it's an equal-opportunity sort of emotion.

Of course, moments of joy that are unshared are not the only time I wish I had a partner. There was a time when I was walking through grief in a few parts of my life, and I would fall asleep on the couch, too exhausted to move my body one more room over to my bed. And to add insult to injury, several nights in a row when I finally did get into my bed, no matter what hour it was, the smoke detectors in my house would start going off, as if to mock me. There was no fire or emergency, and I find that to this day my smoke detectors go off at random times but almost always when I'm overwhelmed or stressed. But in those days of grief? All I knew was the sensation of my body jolting awake out of full slumber and into a fight-or-flight response.

The first night it happened, I covered my ears, full of terror, and when the noise didn't stop, I ran through my bedroom door into the living room and across the kitchen out to the balcony. I called 911 because I didn't know if there was really a fire or not. They came to check things out and discovered the mystery that there was no reason for the alarms to all go off.

The second night it happened, I covered my ears and waited, and the alarms stopped on their own, so I went back to sleep.

The third night that the alarms blared, I remained fairly calm, covering my ears so that I could somehow hear the slow, deep breaths that my therapist had taught me years before, and I shouted a prayer of helplessness into the non-smoky air: "Jesus, I need you to fix this."

Immediately, the alarms stopped.

Though the Lord had come to me in my distress, my body did not get the memo, as tends to be the case. Panic was already a friend of mine from a younger age, but it decided to creep back up every night just before bed to remind me that even if I fell asleep, nothing could stop the possibility of being jolted awake by the smoke detector's blaring alarm and robotic voice literally shouting at me to evacuate. For months, the perceived threat chipped away at my nerves until one day, on a flight through some turbulent weather, fear assigned itself a seat next to mine.

As the plane rocked back and forth in unpredictable sequences, I felt my pulse start to rise and my chest get tight.

I looked to my left and right and was met by strangers. Anxiety was taking over my steadiness, and slowly it leaked all over like a broken pen until I was in a panic. I was moving and I was still. I was clear and everything was a blur. Finally, as the adrenaline slowed down and my pulse began to return to normal, I was overcome by an intense feeling of sadness.

Sadness because I wanted to live a life of adventure, not panic.

Sadness because I wanted to have someone to turn to, and I didn't.

Sadness because I had no choice but to keep moving forward by myself.

Underneath much of our frustration, confusion, and anxiety about singleness, sadness sits, ready to keep us company. We can put up tough facades, believing that courage has to be powerful, and it is! But that doesn't mean it has to be forceful.

This invitation to move graciously through life alone usually gets lost in the mail. There was never a specific moment in which I decided that singleness was exactly what I was hoping for. There was never an announcement made or some sort of resolve that my fate was to be unmarried. It just happened. That's the funny thing about singleness: there's always the potential of meeting a partner, and yet it is never guaranteed. You walk through life by yourself and then one day turn around and realize that you've established patterns and habits and friendships and routines without another person.

Sometimes, bravery is the decision you make because you need to push through a necessary but hard moment. Like with cleaning out a wound, you just suck it up and do the dang thing. The only way out is through, right?

Of course, the way through isn't easy. Singleness is a whole other thing in just about every regard. It's a choice you didn't make. It's a path you didn't decide to walk down. It's a club you didn't sign up for.

And now here we sit, perhaps content for a moment, or perhaps writhing from the pain of it all, and no matter where you are on your route, we all have the same assignment: Keep going.

How do we keep showing up to our lives and not just tolerate them? How do we cry ourselves to sleep and then wake up to go to brunch with friends? How do we attend another wedding and genuinely wish the couple well but get back into our car by ourselves at the end of the night?

Courage is one of those ideas that's often talked about, and we have a general idea of what it is, but I want us to pull apart the meaning of this term for a second.

Perhaps the most memorable instance of the word *courage* in Scripture is from the book of Joshua. If this isn't ringing any bells for you, I'll set the scene.

The enslaved Israelites have fled Egypt and established for themselves a nation of free people. Led by God, they wander out into the wilderness to find the promised land. Along the way, things go sideways multiple times, and God uses different leaders to continue to encourage and guide His people. The first leader, the one who led them out of slavery, is the guy by the name of Moses.

Moses is considered to be one of the greatest leaders of all time in Scripture, and while he is certainly not perfect, he is an incredible example of trusting God and messing up and then coming back to God again. As Moses got older, however, a new leader needed to emerge. We meet Joshua earlier briefly here and there, and Scripture says that he was a man who lingered at the tent where the presence of God was, careful to build his faith.

Exodus 33:11 tells us, "The LORD would speak to Moses face to face, as one speaks to a friend. Then Moses would return to the camp, but his young aide Joshua son of Nun did not leave the tent."

He is one of the young men who showed the most promise to lead next. It wasn't assumed that Joshua would take over, but the Lord spoke to him and told him that he would be next in line.

Multiple times in the beginning of Joshua's ministry, he is given a very specific command to lead the people and is exhorted to be "strong and courageous." This phrase shows up so many times that you know it cannot be an accident or a passing comment. No, this phrase is being used because Joshua is most likely losing his ish and needs to be steadied again. And again. And again.

Joshua had seen what it would cost to lead the people of Israel. Born into slavery in Egypt, he was a young man when Moses led them to freedom. He had witnessed first-hand what happens when the God of miracles shows up. His sandals wore down as he followed a pillar of fire and a pillar of smoke through the desert. He witnessed the Red Sea parting in two, and he collected manna that appeared out of thin air in the desert. He saw the greatness and goodness of God for decades, but he also saw the hard-hearted nature and finicky ways of his brothers and sisters.

He watched as their eyes grew wide with wonder and narrow with suspicion. He saw the wrinkles appear on their faces, and he witnessed them burying their dead as they lived like nomads, with no place to call home. He overheard when they grumbled and whispered that they wished they were back in Egypt just because slavery was predictable. He was there when the people swore that they would turn their hearts back to God, only to watch them swivel their necks and orient their desires to anything that might offer them comfort.

I imagine that Joshua is not only afraid but rightfully weary stepping into this new role. He is wise and he deeply loves God, but he still struggles to feel confident in what the Lord has for him. Knowing full well the weight of leading millions, he is understandably afraid and feeling very uncourageous.

This command that God gives to Joshua to "be strong and courageous" happens three times just in the first chapter of Joshua. Any time that a command or a phrase is repeated, it is meant to be paid attention to. Leading up to the book of Joshua and in the very first paragraphs, it is clear that he is a man in need of steadying. And there are plenty of ways that God could have encouraged him or plenty of advice He could have offered, but instead, He chooses this command.

As always, an opportunity to dig into Hebrew is one of my favorite ways to spend time, so let's take a look at what exactly is being said during these admonitions.

First of all, each time the phrase "be strong and courageous" is used, it's in a grammatical form called the Qal Imperative. This means that it is not a suggestion but a command. It's the difference between "You should go to the store" and "Go to the store—*now*."

The encouragement that God is offering to Joshua is not merely something He wants him to consider, but something

He wants him to immediately take action to do. Now let's look at each of these words, shall we?

The first word, which is translated as "be strong," has to do with strengthening and it is a process. This is not just merely asking him to suck it up, but telling Joshua to actively be strengthened. Other examples of this word can be translated as "to fortify" or "to repair" or "to prevail." This word is often connected to things that get stronger over time like trees or famines. He is being commanded to grow in his strength.

The second word, which is translated as "be courageous," has to do with his posture in that strength. It is to be stout or bold or alert. What I find most interesting, however, is that both of these words often mirror each other. When you put them together, they are "forged together—strengthened," if you will.

You could even translate this phrase as "hold courage and grow courage," or "be courageous and have courage." It is not meant to be redundant, but rather to strengthen the call to be strong. The command itself is acting out what it is commanding Joshua to do.

I wonder what kind of stories were camping out in the back of Joshua's mind as he returned to camp. I can imagine that they were a combination of concern and resolve. Because isn't that the way that we go about being brave? We are simultaneously unsure of everything, and yet something deep in us allows us to be resolved to keep going. This is the mystery of the work of the Holy Spirit in our lives. As single people, we see our bravery reflected in a thousand small decisions as we put one foot in front of the other because there's really no alternative.

Oh, but it certainly doesn't feel like bravery in the moment, does it? It more accurately feels like fear or restlessness, but as time moves forward and we keep journeying along our route, we are choosing to grow good things like kindness and compassion and resolve. Our character is something that, like Joshua's courage, we are holding and growing simultaneously. We do not wake up one day suddenly brave. And we do not wake up one day suddenly content with being single. No, our character and contentedness ebb and flow, developing over time like weather patterns or worn trails that cut through the woods and offer a way forward for others.

And this perhaps is one of the most powerful things about growing the courage to be a single person and exist in the world without apology or desperation or dissatisfaction. As followers of Jesus, we draw from a deeper well, and when we choose to reframe our singleness and our needs as something that is satisfied in the person of Christ, it can be contagious. I'm not saying that we should be showboating about our singleness or bragging to people about how happy we are, because Lord knows people have done that to us and it has been obnoxious. But I am suggesting that when we find Christ to be the truest companion and when we commit to our local church and when we connect to other people and when we communicate what is true and when we draw near in closeness and commiseration in healthy ways, there is an opportunity to push forward with courage.

And courage is contagious. Your peace will preach.

A lot of us have grown into single adults with few blueprints of what that looks like in a joyful and healthy and honest way. We were handed books about singleness that treated the topic as though it were a problem to be solved.

We were given resources on how to be more dateable or told to put ourselves out there. For many of us, our whole lives have consisted of people trying to fix something that God has handed us on purpose. He has not forgotten about us. He has not let us slip through the cracks.

Listen to me when I tell you this: You are not single for any reason other than that you are single. You are not single because you are unlovable or because you are too much or not enough. You are not single because you have disappointed Jesus. You are not single because you are ugly. You are not single because you are too jacked up from your own trauma or experiences to be in a healthy relationship.

The moment we start playing games to figure out a solution to our circumstances as if that will fix our broken hearts, we lose out. We have to stop comparing ourselves to our married friends and wondering what the formula is to get a band on that left-hand finger. We have to end the narrative that our singleness is a curse or a punishment. We have to step bravely forward and be courageous enough to say things like:

I am single and I am loved.

I am single and I am seen.

I am single and I am cherished.

I am single and I am lonely.

I am single and I really need a hug.

When we choose to voice what is happening in our heads and our hearts and we choose to walk in the direction of community instead of isolation, we are living courageously. And it will only happen by the grace of God.

Happiness and positive vibes get us further in this culture, and I recognize the reality that it is easier to listen to somebody go on and on about how they can fix our problems rather than to sit down and try to decipher what is true in the mess of the lies we have been told our entire lives. Every single day I lament that people are walking around Barnes & Noble looking for a resource that is going to help them stop being single as if ending singleness is the endgame.

You, beloved of God, are worth more than that.

You are called to walk as if you are going somewhere good.

As if you are already somewhere that is good.

It's hard to believe in the goodness of where we are when we feel the things that we lack. I am not suggesting that our understanding of goodness results in constantly being happy or grateful or even content. No, goodness exists whether or not we feel it. Because God is good and His character does not change, remember? Sometimes, we just need a different perspective.

Back in 2015, I was faced with the challenge of moving across the country to work for a nonprofit that I really admired. It was an internship that was funded by donors, so I had to write letters and ask people for financial help, which was humbling in and of itself, but I also was notoriously bad at any kind of fundraiser. In elementary school, when they gave you the giant box of candy to sell, I don't think I ever sold more than one bar, and I had to give it all back.

Later on, when I had an opportunity to raise funds again, it did not work. Maybe I just didn't have the marketing chops for it, but when I found out that what was standing between me and this internship was fundraising, I lost hope immediately.

When I finally decided to make a plan, I chose to build a team of support that would not only provide financial means (which I practically needed to make the internship happen) but ultimately prayer and actual community. What was supposed to take all summer to accomplish ended up being completed within seven weeks. I was fully funded and had over two hundred people on my prayer support team.

These people and these friendships kept me afloat when I was struggling the most with loneliness and feeling overwhelmed that year of ministry. But the thing that got me over the line from despair to hope was a moment I had with God right before I sent out any letters or emails asking for help.

It was the end of my last semester of seminary, and I knew that after a very challenging year, I was about to walk into a summer with the same intensity. I had sustained several losses over the course of the previous months, and I was limping into a season that I knew I was going to need energy for. Fundraising and community building are not for the faint of heart. As winter gave way to spring and I prepared for my summer of letter writing and phone calls, I decided to take a drive one afternoon and it led me to a side road about twenty miles from my house. As I turned down a gravel road, it eventually became dirt and then mostly potholes. I expertly maneuvered around them, as I grew up on a dirt road, and at the very end of a wooded trail, I found myself at the end of a peninsula of sorts.

There was no one around, and I felt an invitation from the Lord to leave my phone and my keys behind and just go be present with Him. It seemed silly, but I decided to listen. As I walked, I was surrounded by woodland, and it felt like a metaphor for where my heart was. I was unable to see very far in front of me and I felt like I was aching for some kind of long-distance view, but it just didn't exist.

The trees were too dense to get a vision of what was going on ahead of me. All that I saw were leaves and brush and a wall of tree trunks. As I ventured down the short path, my weariness gave way to wonder as I turned the last bend and found myself standing right at the edge of the Great Marsh.

For miles and miles, there were no trees or obstacles, and I could see the tidal estuary sneaking around the beautiful grass, carving its way from the ocean to where I stood. I did not hear the audible voice of God, but I could sense in my spirit that He was offering a new perspective. After what felt like forever walking through the woods in my own heart, I was now standing in the wide-open expanse that led to even wider expanses, and I found my heart encouraged to recall that there are still wide-open places, even when we do not find ourselves standing near them.

During so much of our lives as single people, we find ourselves walking in the woods, unsure of what's around the next corner. Will I still be single this time next year? Am I going to have children or will I get older until I can't? If the person that I'm dating turns out to not be the right one, did I waste my time?

Despite my love of '90s lady country music, the majority of our singleness doesn't feel like wide-open spaces. Our eyes tend to adjust to a myopic view of the world around us, and we forget that there is a wide-open world just on the other side of whatever we are facing at the moment.

When we wander through the woodlands long enough, it's easy to lose courage. The default can be to shrink until we are groping our way through branches and brush, unsure where the joy went.

Exploration is no longer fun when you're lost in the woods. Let's go back to the idea of the route. If this were hiking, we would need to be prepared. And part of preparation is having the right tools for the journey. For example, if I know that I'm going to be alone for a significant stretch of time, I will schedule catch-up phone calls with good friends or make sure I have people who are checking in on me. A little extra effort goes far in this area, and I have found that there's a great chance to reconnect with friends by calling them on long road trips and lunchtime walks.

It's also really key that people know when you are struggling and feeling a lack of courage. Sometimes we front that we are a lot better than we actually are. Just because we showed up to a party doesn't mean it was easy to get out of bed. Just because we seem okay doesn't mean it's not taking a herculean effort.

Thankfully for us as Christians, we are not solely responsible for mustering up courage or giving ourselves a pep talk that's going to inspire us to face another day with gumption and grace. No, we get to go straight to the source and ask God to give us our courage.

Sometimes, when I'm not sure exactly how to do that, I come up with simple refrains that I can repeat as a prayer throughout my day. When I don't see how God can be in a situation that feels overwhelming, I say things like, "Jesus, I know you're near in this. Show me where you are," or "God, You are ever-present. Help me to not feel alone." These statements feel really basic, but they get to the heart of what we are experiencing. I don't know about you, but I can be a real overthinker, and so simple prayers like these often go a long way to cut straight to how I'm feeling and ask the Lord to be near. Because the more that we notice His nearness, the steadier we get.

And beyond that, when we are steady in our own hearts and minds, there is an opportunity to be steady for others. I have walked through losses in my life that felt so isolating and rare, and I often thought that maybe those losses set me aside from the larger community or made me stand out in some way that was more of a curse than a blessing. There was a period of time in which I felt like my actual presence would bum people out because so much was going wrong. At my lowest, I was jobless, financially depleted, and searching for plane tickets that I could not afford so that I could cross the country for the memorial service of a beloved friend who I had just had the honor of walking with as she met Jesus.

One morning, I received a text from a friend who herself had walked through deep heartache, and she offered me her frequent flier miles, which allowed me to go and honor my dearly departed companion.

She understood that I needed strength, and she lent hers to me.

I recently received a text from one of my best friends from college and he asked if I could send him a prayer from the book *Every Moment Holy*.[1] He specifically wanted the one titled "A Prayer for Dying Well," and I knew that his father, who had recently started hospice, was nearing the end. A few hours later, his father found himself in eternity, leaning on the breast of Jesus.

I do not know what the coming weeks and months will be like for my friends who are lamenting the loss of a parent, but I do know from experience that they will need courage.

And this is what's wild about our moments of fear or panic or total overwhelm: They somehow give us the capacity to have compassion and care for others further down the road. I don't believe that God allows hard and horrific things to happen to us just to teach us some sort of cosmic lesson, but I do believe that on this side of eternity, where grief is inevitable and fear is tangible and the insecurities we carry are prevalent, it is no small grace that we can look around to our community and see evidence of the Lord's faithfulness and have it bolster our faith.

Courage never feels courageous when it's happening. It feels terribly lonely and uncertain and makes us feel small. But when I am certain that it's time to curl up into a ball, I ask Jesus for the stamina to reach out in the right direction. Sometimes the reach is for support from others, and sometimes the reach is an extension to someone else caught in the depths of discouragement.

When our matches are soaking wet and there's no dry ground, courage is the belief that it's possible to still spark a small flame. And that little flame can be nourished and given oxygen until it becomes steady over time. It is tender and feels fickle at first, just a flicker of bravery here and there. But as it grows and expands and finds room to burn, it gives light to everyone else.

What if your courageous act of living intentionally as a single person and taking trips and staying present when you want to check out ultimately reminds others that singleness is not a death sentence?

Perhaps you haven't had an example of how to live a life of faithfulness as a single person. A lot of what makes this an uphill battle is that singleness culturally seems to be the exception more than the rule. Even if people are not getting married, plenty of them have a partner or are regularly dating, and it can make us feel left behind.

There is a phrase in the writing community that goes, "Write the book you wish had been written for you."

If there isn't a clear map, what if *you* are a mapmaker? If there isn't a trail, perhaps you're part of a team that makes one. If there isn't a guide, maybe your words and experiences will allow someone to walk the terrain of singleness without getting as lost as you did. I'm not saying that it is our responsibility to make other people's experience of singleness one that is healthy and good, *but what if it is*? What if, as people committed to community, we are responsible for the holistic future of the church by carrying courage and making a new way forward?

I dream of a world in which people in the church borrow the courage of those who have gone before and no longer feel overwhelmed by the reality of being single. That they have an imagination for a life of meaning and thriving and they don't feel the same overwhelm we do when making big life transitions. That they have a way forward into whatever comes their way because they were taught that a life of singleness takes extra effort but is not impossible.

We are the ones who can widen the perspective of the local church and the communities we live in. We can be honest about what hurts and tell stories of what we've learned. We can find our voices and even laugh in the face of the voice that says, "You're all alone and always will be." And each day that we choose to enrich our lives and refuse to wave a white flag of surrender to despair is a day won.

We are the ones who can, like Joshua, hold courage and grow courage. We can make friends and laugh hard and give often and pray passionately and host graciously and welcome others and declare hope.

Like any endeavor of this sort, there's no way this is going to be easy. There is no way it's going to be straightforward and endlessly fun, and there's also no way that it's regularly going to feel worth it. But so much of my life has been spent wishing someone would lend me their courage. Maybe it's time to find our steady anchor in Jesus and refuse to be robbed of our testimony of what the Lord can do when we trust that He is trustworthy.

nine

Community

Last year, my church in New England started the tradition of going on a retreat. It had happened in the past but had not always been consistent, and they decided to bring it back. We drove two hours up to a camp in New Hampshire in the off-season and spent two and a half days together among the changing leaves and crisp weather. We shared s'mores and stories and meals and games, and it felt like a big family vacation in many ways.

This church was a home to me in troubled seasons during grad school, and when I moved from Tennessee back to Massachusetts, I knew I needed to be with them. They had been a support system of prayer over the years, and when I lived away, I would regularly go back to visit. So regularly, in fact, that when I went to ask if I needed to become a member a second time (since I'd moved away four years earlier), they said, "Well, in the bylaws, if you're present at least every few months, you retain membership. And we forgot to take you off the list. Plus, you showed up frequently enough that I suppose we just kept you. You're already a member."

I recognize that it is a gift to be known by a church in this way. This is not the story for many people. There are scandals and disagreements and abuse and neglect. Leaders fail and sin runs rampant, tearing through the town and leaving devastation behind. Congregants don't treat one another with compassion and make room for plenty of disregard. Cliques form and people get siloed. People walk into a place that is meant to be a place of belonging, and they are met with a lack of hospitality or are just ignored completely. This is discouraging because it actually communicates that it doesn't matter whether they walk through the doors or not.

But I need you to know this: It very much so matters if you walk through the doors, because you belong in the community of faith, and we need you to get over here.

If you have found yourself restless or unsettled or wounded by those in your local church, first of all, I want to tell you that I'm sorry that this heartbreaking reality is one that you have known all too well. I'm sorry that you were not greeted and no one invited you to sit with them and you were not seen when you were already going out on a limb, vulnerably trying to join something bigger than yourself. You did a brave thing, and it was not met with the honor it deserved.

When it comes to building community, there is a whole lot of tenderness involved that is not always seen and understood. So as we lay out what a community could look like, I want to acknowledge that what you have experienced is not necessarily what could happen everywhere. There are churches that preach from the Word of God and open their doors and live as if they are delighted to be together. There are pastors who counsel well and give biblical insight that allows people to thrive. There are people who show up for one another and fight to build reconciliation and are deeply committed to seeing the movement of God in their local context.

Turns out, the church is made up of a whole lot of people, and all of us are human. All of us fall short from time to time and do things and say things that we may or may not regret. Some will repent of these sins and turn back and be better members of the church community. But the truth is that not everyone will, and you can meet some really dicey people within the four walls of the local church.

We serve a very good God who does not change and is perfect in every way, but we also sit in pews alongside other human beings who don't always represent Him well.

Each Sunday is an opportunity for us to learn how to be more like Christ and live like Him, and though it is tricky, it is possible to experience what we call the "now and not yet." To experience a taste of what heaven could be and still be in the messy middle. The work of God is being done, but it is not fully realized.

We live in the middle of this now and not yet, feeling in our hearts and minds that we belong but still struggling to feel we belong.

We are sinners saved by grace right now, but we still sin. We battle the flesh and struggle with addiction and our own shortcomings.

We are able to love our neighbors right now, but we also cannot solve every problem, and there are times when we drop the ball in our relationships.

We can experience the peace of Jesus right now, and it cannot be explained by the outside world, but true and lasting peace and a world without trouble is not yet here until Jesus comes to make all things new.

If we can accept the reality of the now and not yet, we can live as a people who have hope, even in the midst of crumbling circumstances. We are able to reach out in friendship, even when we have been burned, and we are able, by the grace of God, to start new when all feels lost.

A glimpse of the goodness of community was what I found during our church retreat, not because it was perfect or stressless, but because it was simple and honest, and we pointed each other toward Jesus.

A few times a day, we would gather in a chapel that had walls of windows and felt like a cathedral right in the middle of nature. Outside, the wind would blow the leaves and give us a display of creation that was stunning. Inside, we heard testimonies from other church members of how God had met them at different points in their lives and we sang worship songs and we heard from our leaders about how we as a church belong to one another and ultimately to God, and that was stunning too. For a few days, our routes all converged, and we welcomed one another and were able to behold the work God was doing in each of us.

As our pastor, Bobby, shared about this vision of Christian community, he was verklempt, one of my favorite qualities about him. He regularly tears up when he considers the beauty of God and His story. Bobby is relentlessly sappy in the best ways and leads us out of a hard-fought faith. He has experienced heartache unlike many I know, and it leads him over and over again toward tenderness when it could make him bitter and hard-hearted.

A few years ago, the church leaders decided to give Bobby a sabbatical as he approached nine years of ministry at the church. They wanted to plan ahead, so we had a town hall–style meeting to talk about what this could look like. How would we as a small church function without our pastor for three months? Bobby was happy with any kind of reprieve after a heavy and exhausting few years, and person after person stood up, thanked him for his ministry, and then said wild things like, "A year is a long time to wait for a break. Can we give him a few weeks off now?" In a time of burnout among ministry leaders, this posture our church took moved me. We saw him not only as our pastor but as our brother.

When Bobby was on his sabbatical, congregants stepped in to care for one another and local pastors did pulpit supply, making sure that someone was preaching truth every Sunday. Church staff filled in the big gaps, and it allowed Bobby to be cared for because no one was allowed to reach out to him for church business. And beyond that? As a church, we did a summer series on why rest was important so we could all grow spiritually alongside him and his family.

It is no wonder he often talks about community and love and encouragement with tears in his eyes—we all do.

And as we sat in that chapel at the retreat and he shared from a weary, presabbatical perspective, everyone bore witness to it. Kids had a setup in the back of the room so they could overhear the good story of the gospel and soak in its truth while they played with blocks and coloring books.

One adult volunteer in the back was working with the children and watched his wife effortlessly help a kid glue some felt together for a craft, and he said to me, "Man, I just don't know what to do with kids."

"Just talk to them like people," I suggested.

I watched him step forward, lower to his knees, and say, "Do you want help with this?" to a little girl who was struggling with too much glue and not enough felt.

This, too, is community building. When we think of our work as a church, it is vital that we remember that all of us belong in a church community, but that doesn't mean we always get to a place of feeling that immediately. Yes, married people, families, single individuals, and children are all welcome to participate. In fact, we need everyone to participate.

Once, during a meeting about our annual budget, we were talking about the youth budget, and a mom stood up and said, "Yes, let's be sure to invest in the next generation with a good budget for the youth group, but we have to remember that when our students participate in worship ministry or help with the nursery or learn from our elderly members, that invests in the next generation too. Youth ministry is more than just the youth group. And when we give to worship ministry or elder care events, we *are* giving to the youth."

This is a beautiful outlook, and we work to make it a reality, but what does that look like practically? After all, I can say that I belong and you belong, but the experiences we have and the culture we create make the difference. We have to look at what Jesus sets forth for the culture of His people by seeing how He responds in the most dire circumstances. What does He make a priority? What does He care about as He's in His final moments before death?

For context, Jesus was the firstborn son of His family, which meant that He was responsible for caring for His mother. Without Him, she might be destitute and without support.

His father, Joseph, is never mentioned, so it's safe to assume he has died. This means she would be without her firstborn son and also a widow, the most vulnerable combination in her culture.

Jesus looks to His disciple, John, who stands next to a weeping mother Mary. Jesus is hanging and bleeding, and inhaling while being crucified is enormously painful. This is because you are held up by your feet on a tiny piece of wood, and as you lose your strength, your body pulls down and you start to suffocate. The only way to breathe is to push up using your nailed-through feet and gasp. Jesus musters His strength, bears down, and pushes up with agony, inhaling, and Scripture says,

> When Jesus saw his mother there, and the disciple whom he loved standing nearby, he said to her, "Woman, here is your son," and to the disciple, "Here is your mother." From that time on, this disciple took her into his home. (John 19:26–27)

This moment of Jesus providing for His mother shows that in the family of God, we cross familial lines and care for those who are next to us as if we are blood. The church is not just about being friendly or welcoming, but about being in a community that gives and receives and provides and cherishes. Practically speaking, we are to treat one another with dignity and care and actual support, not only offering well-wishes or platitudes.

We aren't just neighbors; we are households. When one celebrates, we all do. And when one of us suffers, we all do. No matter our relationship status or generation, we are part of one body. Recently, we gave the third graders at our church Bibles of their very own. It's the age when they get to stop going to children's church and become full participants in the sermon part of the service.

As the students stood, gripping their hardcover NIV Adventure Bibles (a true Baptist rite of passage), our children's director joyfully proclaimed, "When you pass the peace to one another, do not pass it above their heads to their parents only. Their milestones are our milestones."

My friend Maggie Freeman often says, "Revival starts at home." And she's right. The work of community has to begin right where we stand, not somewhere far away.

I get to participate in my church with a sense of joy and welcome right here, right now. I get to celebrate alongside brothers and sisters when we welcome new babies and college students who just arrived for school and curious passersby who saw the parking lot fill up at the same time each weekend. I get to greet old friends and young kids as equal parts of the church.

I'm not going to pretend that it's always simple and rosy. Every family, whether full of major trauma or not, is complicated. Which means that every church, riddled with scandal and drama or not, is complicated. Being a "family" of sorts does not mean that we ignore abuse or unhealthy habits, but rather the opposite. We are meant to be so committed to one another that we encourage behavior that is good and right and aligns with the values of the gospel. One of the reasons I believe God gave us this imagery of being brothers and sisters of faith (Heb. 10:19; Matt. 12:48–50) is because there is a level of commitment that is more intimate than that of casual friendship. If the church is only a gathering of acquaintances, we can come and go as we please and we owe much less to one another. However, if we take the truth of Scripture seriously, we actually belong to one another in a way that is sacred.

There are more passages of Scripture about adoption than there are about other popular theological topics like justification or sanctification. God is referred to as our Father and it is very much so on purpose. His relationship with us is one of a parent, and we are considered not only children of God but coheirs with one another. No one is elevated above another. We are all seen as those who inherit what He offers. God is not choosing favorite kids or suggesting that anyone is too wayward to come forward. No, Scripture shows us that even those who are rebellious and lost can be welcomed back.

The well-known story of the prodigal son in Luke 15 reminds us that the heart of a good father isn't in keeping score but is certainly in keeping the door open for when a child is ready to come back home. The story of Joseph in Genesis 37–50 highlights the truth that even when our families betray us in the most intense ways, we can extend grace to them and find a healing way forward. Of course, there are also plenty of stories of families who could not get on the same page. And some of them were these very same stories!

In the parable of the prodigal son, the brother who had played by the family rules is incredibly jealous and bitter toward the brother who rebelled. Before they were reconciled, Joseph's brothers sold him into slavery and abused him and tried to steal what was rightfully his. Though we are siblings, our sinful nature makes the possibility of reconciliation much more complex. Sometimes, damage is done in a way that cannot be resolved on this side of heaven.

Sometimes, people never see a way forward toward forgiveness and people do not repent of the sin that has entangled them.

Still, even as we grieve these things, we do not grieve as those with no hope (1 Thess. 4:13). A passage of Scripture that I regularly come back to says in as much as it is possible, live at peace with one another (Rom. 12:18). This offers us the caveat that sometimes the disagreement is too deep, but still, we need to do our part of trying to live at peace with one another and trying to reconcile what we can.

If you are in relationships that have been broken so severely that they cannot be mended, my prayer is that the Reconciler will minister to your heart and bring you to a place of acceptance and wholeness despite what is missing. The only One who can truly reconcile us to Himself and to one another is Christ, and it's very possible that as we live in the tension of the now and not yet, we have to painfully embrace that we do not know how things are going to end up and we do not know if they will ever see resolution in this lifetime and we do not know how the story will unfold. Still, we are invited to be part of the family of God and to live at peace and in unity and to persist in this life as if our faith is true and our God is real and our calling allows us to do life together. Truly together.

I am in my midthirties, and one of my favorite things about this season is the fact that I am young enough to remember what it's like to be a wild child and also an angsty teenager and also an insecure twentysomething. I am more set in my ways now as a result of what the Lord has carried me through and, seventeen years into legal adulthood, I'm starting to get a little bit of the rhythm of what it means to be a grown-up. I have friends who are single and I have friends who are newlyweds and I have friends who are celebrating decades and decades together. I have friends who are retired and I have friends who are searching for jobs and I have friends who are not legally old enough to have a job yet.

If I am going to live in the community of faith, I have to engage with the community of faith. When I walk in the doors of my church, I have to be ready to relate to anyone I come across as if their story matters and their experience matters—because it does. It matters what they are facing at work or at home. It matters that they are overjoyed or downtrodden. Part of existing together is inviting others in and proclaiming, "Get over here! We need you—even in this state."

The other day, I asked a six-year-old what her favorite part of being six was, and she told me very confidently that it was being small so she could hide and jump out and scare her dad. We proceeded to have a whole conversation about how true that is, and I never once asked her about her future goals or told her to take things more seriously. To her, this was the primary thing to be discussed.

She reminds me that being playful is a good thing, and what I love is that she sees herself in relation to her father who is twenty-seven years older than her. She sees herself in relation to the community she is a part of.

There is a girl at my church who likes to read the little paper church directory for fun and makes sure to send cards to the people she knows on their birthdays. Since the address and birthday of the person are listed, it makes this task very easy.

Recently my dad, who is seventy years old, told me that my twelve-year-old niece wanted to make some money, and he has a hard time keeping his schedule in order, so he tells her when his doctor's appointments or different engagements that he may have on his calendar are, and she calls him the day before to remind him of what's coming.

I know grandparents who have given their retirement years to moving closer to family so they can help their children raise the next generation. I know teenagers who like to help people move because they think it's genuinely enjoyable to carry boxes up stairs. I know young professionals who are being mentored by business owners in their sixties. And all of them relate to one another with so much joy because they see that the world is, in fact, widened when we come together.

God is not casual about how we are called to dwell together. In fact, community is the thing that consistently points us back to Jesus. When I am among brothers and sisters in Christ and I face something that is exhausting or heartbreaking or overwhelming, they are the ones who are going to pray over me and offer encouragement and send me Scripture. In the last two hours, two different people have texted me because they heard I was going to be writing, and they wanted me to know that they were praying for me. I tell you this not to show off my community as much as to expand your imagination as to how we can live this out practically.

If you know someone who is struggling, send them a text message telling them that you are not only aware of it but you are also praying for them and want to help.

If you know someone who is getting married soon, reach out and ask if there are ways you can help with the planning process or be an extra set of hands to pull together the final details.

If you know someone who is getting ready to retire and will likely feel restless, ask them how you can support them in this season and maybe invite them over for lunch as their days are going to be a little bit more flexible.

If you know someone who hasn't been to church in a while and you've been wondering how they're doing, swing by their house and drop off a jar of flowers with a note telling them you're praying for them. It's so simple to live out a spirit of generosity and hospitality.

And my prayer is that you, too, will actively receive from others a sense of welcome. You are a valuable part of the global church and deserve to be seen and known and to actively participate in your local expression of the church. You should be able to walk down the aisle and look for a seat and be invited in. You deserve to be fully at home in holy community.

The early church was known for gathering and breaking bread and reading Scripture and praying and worshiping together. And these are all things we can still do today! We can still ask people to join for dinner and we can still get really bold and invite one another to be intentional in prayer and Scripture reading. We can send one another favorite Bible verses. We can share favorite recipes. We can ask that teenager who is learning to play the guitar if they will strum out a few hymns or familiar songs so you can all sing off-tune together.

A few Sundays ago, Bobby shared about how aspen trees exist in a network. Usually, a tree will have roots that dig deep into the ground, but not aspens. I did some research and here is what I found from the National Forest Foundation:

One aspen tree is actually only a small part of a larger organism. A stand or group of aspen trees is considered a singular organism with the main life force underground in the extensive root system. Before a single aspen trunk appears above the surface, the root system may lie dormant for many years until the conditions are just right, including sufficient sunlight. In a single stand, each tree is a genetic replicate of the other, hence the name a "clone" of aspens used to describe a stand.

Older than the massive Sequoias or the biblical Bristlecone Pines, the oldest known aspen clone has lived more than 80,000 years on Utah's Fishlake National Forest. Not only is the clone the oldest living organism, weighing in at an estimated 6,600 tons, it is also the heaviest. Even if the trees of a stand are wiped out, it is very difficult to permanently extinguish an aspen's root system due to the rapid rate in which it reproduces.[1]

The way that we gather together on a Sunday doesn't look that different from what may have happened twenty years ago or fifty years ago or three hundred years ago. The way that we break bread together and share meals could also be seen a thousand years ago on the other side of the world. The way that we have long conversations late into the night and hold hands, interceding and praying for peace, is a tradition that dates back for generations and millennia. It is difficult for anything else to be the case just because we are part of a long story that has extensive roots.

I know that as a single person, there is a very real temptation to pull ourselves away from others. I know that it's not always magic, and people say things that make us feel small or unseen in a way that has us inching toward the exit.

I know that people have been unkind, and it doesn't matter whether they did it intentionally or not because we are still lying awake at night thinking about it.

I have been told that I don't know how to care for kids because I don't have any of my own. I've been told that I'm not putting myself out there enough and need to try harder in order to be in a relationship. I've been told that I cannot give any kind of relationship advice until I'm married.

But this is the thing: None of us have ever been in one another's shoes, and yet we have so many similar experiences and our stories overlap much more than we realize at first glance. As I have wandered through these years with no wedding ring on my finger, I have found that deep down, we are all looking for the same needs to be met.

I need companionship and so do my married friends.

I need commiseration and so do my married friends.

I need connection and so do my married friends.

I need commitment and so do my married friends.

I need communication and so do my married friends.

I need consistency and so do my married friends.

I need closeness and so do my married friends.

I need courage and so do my married friends.

I need community and so do my married friends.

We have been told that we're not in the same stage or season and we don't have things in common, when we're all out here struggling with the same longings and callings and feelings that we just don't have enough.

If married people belong in church, we do too.

We're out here with empty hands and full hands and hopeful hearts and grieving hearts, and all I know is that

Jesus gave us the gift of one another. It is not an accident that you ended up in the places you've ended up.

No, the God of the universe who is completely sovereign has, by His grace, dropped you right into your neighborhood. He has brought you to this place in your career. He has surrounded you with these friends and this local church. And while some of those things may shift over time, there is always an opportunity to dig deeper into community as a way of understanding how God has created us to work.

All of us have a place to sit.

Building a good and beautiful life that is rich and full of relationships is not something that is only for those who are experiencing a lifelong partner. As single people, our perspective is vital to understanding the complexity of the human experience. What we proclaim from our route of singleness will bolster the faith of others and help them see how good Jesus is and how near His comfort can be. When we allow our stories to unfold as though they are not a mistake, everyone benefits.

The story has to stop being about what's wrong with us and shift to what is redeemed and right in us. You are not single because you've lost out on goodness. You are single because your good God who loves you deeply has allowed that to be the case. And His love is no less fierce, and His affection is not withheld.

It is currently 6:48 a.m. And I'm sitting in my childhood bedroom, thinking about what it has been like for these thirty-five years of never having been married. I have ten nieces and nephews and my siblings have been married for long enough that it's hard to remember what life was like before they brought their partners into the family. My oldest niece is nearly thirteen and my youngest is only three and a half months old.

There have certainly been times that have been challenging and lonely as my friends and family got married and started their lives with someone committed to them in this formal way. There have certainly been times when I have been frustrated and confused about the fact that I never got married young and would never be able to either. There have certainly been moments when I felt unqualified to be surrounded by so many kids and involved in so many conversations about relationships.

Still, as I wait for the youngest ones to wake up and come and find me this morning, I wonder what their lives will hold. Statistically, a few of them will probably not get married until they're a little older. Maybe some of them will be single for their entire lives. And if that's the case, I will be here to tell them this truth:

Jesus is good and He delights in you in a way that you will never be able to get to the bottom of. You can try your hardest to figure out what you've done wrong to be single, but the fact of the matter is that He has given you this route to travel, and He also has no intention of leaving you to travel alone. There are going to be days when you feel that you cannot put one foot in front of the other, but there are also going to be days when you see things that are stunning and wild and absolutely breathtaking.

This route that you travel is not one that is effortless, but it is also one that is possible to trek. Some of the most faithful Christians have never felt the coolness of metal around their ring finger, but they *have* felt the embrace of Christ as they venture forward, understanding intimacy with Him in a way that many will not know until forever.

The church that you attend and the office that you go to and the home that you make are all full of the goodness of God, and you belong in the places that He has faithfully brought you to. You have not missed out on something else because of your relationship status. You have not fallen behind in life because of your relationship status. You are not failing at being an adult because of your relationship status. No, this place where you are is so good and can be so full.

I know that there are days you want to give in and go find a partner that you can settle down with just for the sake of settling down. But I am also here to tell you that it never works out when we take things into our own hands. Savor your singleness. Ask your friends to remind you that it is a good thing. Give them the bolt cutters and allow them to rescue you from yourself on dark days. And write things down if you can so that you can look back and watch the ways that the Lord moves even when you feel like everyone is moving on without you.

We need you in the community of God. We need your voice and we need your testimony and we need your perspective to flourish. Don't give up and go quietly. Don't give in and walk away.

My life has not gone the way I thought on nearly every front, and I have no idea what the coming years will bring me. But I can promise you that singleness is not a curse, and no matter what happens, I will shout these words until my voice gives out:

You who are feeling outcast.

You who are unsure if you belong.

You who genuinely believe that we would be better off apart from one another.

Come join in. Come share your story. Come build something good.

You are loved and seen, friend.

Get over here.

Acknowledgments

Each time I sit down to write acknowledgments, I want to make a list of roughly one thousand people who have made writing possible. I know now that I will never get everyone by name, but you bet I'm going to try.

Thank you to my churches who have always preached that I was an equal part of the community even though I wasn't married. You dignified me from the pulpit and in practice, and I am forever thankful for it.

Thank you to my family who have always made sure I felt included and have always answered graciously when the kids ask why I'm not married yet.

Thank you to my counselors and mentors and those who have offered so much support and wisdom over the years, especially about this topic.

Thank you to my friends who have cheered me on and supported this work.

When I signed my contract, you signed it too.

Thank you to Bob and Nancy Stallard and Eliza and Brooks Lemmon for lending me your spaces to process and write and pace all while recovering from mono and finishing this book.

You opened your home, and it made all the difference.

Thank you to those who brought meals and prayed and helped carry my exhausted frame across the finish line: my (in)courage sisters, Kevin, Bailey, Bobby, Julie, Tim, Ann, Jordan, Matt, Laura, Clay, Sarah B., Sarah S., Amy, Annalise, Dawn, Cathy, Lissa, Savannah, Heather, Shelley, De, Sue, Debbie, Patti, Barb, Valerie, Kristine, Christy, Nicole, Annie, Lisa, Sharon, Maddie, Liz, Megan, Eliza, Rachel, Rebecca, Shauna A., Shauna K., Adam, Maggie, Kelsea, Noel, Tracey, Ted, Beth, Jim, Ellie, JJ, Clarissa, Brad, Gina, Adam, Enid, Richard, Devin, Becki, Ken, Emma, Matt, Cathy, and Ken.

Thank you to the team at Revell (Wendy, Lauren, and many others!). And thank you to Grace P. Cho for taking my mess of words and helping foster them into an actual book.

And thank you to Ali Bitzer, Corrine Grant, Natalie Crowson, Jana Holiday, Gwen McWhorter, Taylor Leonhardt, Ivette Garcia, Kristine Rego, Kristin Beattie, Rachel Dean, Laura Gallant, Alycia Thornton, Dawn Bryden, Monie Fluth, Lauren Purdy, Melody Chan, Shannon Read, Dan Grant, Heidi Olson, Ian Black, T. J. Ono, Ricky Shille, Matthew Ronan, Bre Lee, Christen Bohanon, Annie F. Downs, Katy Boatman, Jordyn Perry, Kaitlyn Bouchillon, Aliza Latta, Barb Roose, Karina Allen, Amanda Becton, Maria Reiss, Stephanie Duncan, Kristin Gelinas, Talia Messina, Amanda Privett, Lianna Sours, Kate Hayashi, Daphne Bamburg, Sam Littlefield, Lyndsey Sweeney, Heidi Shorts, Maggie Freeman, and so many others who have reminded me of the beauty of living fully and looking to Jesus.

I love you all. You show me the kingdom.

Notes

Introduction

1. "Malunion Fracture," *Boston Children's Hospital*, accessed August 18, 2024, https://www.childrenshospital.org/conditions/malunion-fracture.

Chapter 1 Companionship

1. Kenneth Grahame and Arthur Rackham, *The Wind in the Willows: An Illustrated Classic* (Canterbury Classics, 2017), 80.
2. Grahame and Rackham, *Wind in the Willows*, 80–81.

Chapter 2 Commiseration

1. Paige Benton, "Singled Out by God for Good," *PCPC Witness*, February 1998, https://static.pcpc.org/articles/singles/singledout.pdf.
2. "Can't Help Myself," track 3 on Sandra McCracken, *In Feast or Fallow*, 2010.

Chapter 3 Connection

1. Ann-Marie Widström et al., "Skin-to-Skin Contact the First Hour After Birth, Underlying Implications and Clinical Practice," *Acta paediatrica* 108, no. 7 (March 2019), https://www.ncbi.nlm.nih.gov/pmc/articles/PMC6949952/.
2. Widström et al., "Skin-to-Skin Contact."
3. "The Trends Redefining Romance Today," *Barna Group*, February 9, 2017, https://www.barna.com/research/trends-redefining-romance-today/.
4. *APA Dictionary of Psychology*, "social," updated April 19, 2018, https://dictionary.apa.org/social.
5. "Here's How Social Media Affects Your Mental Health," *McLean Hospital*, March 29, 2024, https://www.mcleanhospital.org/essential/it-or-not-social-medias-affecting-your-mental-health.

6. "The Bridge," track 3 on Taylor Leonhardt, *Hold Still*, 2021.

7. *APA Dictionary of Psychology*, "prosocial," updated April 19, 2018, https://dictionary.apa.org/prosocial.

Chapter 4 Commitment

1. "Expedition," track 2 on Sara Groves, *Floodplain*, Sponge Records, 2015.

Chapter 5 Communication

1. Thomas L. Constable, "Luke 22:61–62," Constable's Notes on Luke 22, NET Bible, accessed September 14, 2024, netbible.org/bible/Luke+22#.

2. Gloria Mark, Daniela Gudith, and Ulrich Klocke, "The Cost of Interrupted Work: More Speed and Stress," *Donald Bren School of Information and Computer Sciences*, January 24, 2008, https://ics.uci.edu/~gmark/chi08-mark.pdf.

Chapter 7 Closeness

1. "The Often-Overlooked Importance of Physical Intimacy | Tips from The Family Institute," *The Family Institute*, March 22, 2018, https://www.family-institute.org/behavioral-health-resources/magic-touch.

2. Lauren F. Winner, *Real Sex: The Naked Truth about Chastity* (Brazos, 2006), 37.

3. Gary Chapman, *The 5 Love Languages: The Secret to Love that Lasts* (Northfield Publishing, 2024).

Chapter 8 Courage

1. Douglas Kaine McKelvey, *Every Moment Holy, Volume 2: Death, Grief, and Hope* (Rabbit Room Press, 2021).

Chapter 9 Community

1. Hannah Featherman, "Tree Profile: Aspen—So Much More Than a Tree," *National Forest Foundation* (blog), acessed August 19, 2024, https://www.nationalforests.org/blog/tree-profile-aspen-so-much-more-than-a-tree.

Melissa Zaldivar is the author of *Kingdom Come* and *What Cannot Be Lost* and host of the *Cheer Her On* podcast. She holds a master's in theology from Gordon-Conwell Theological Seminary and lives in New England. You can usually find her looking for a good sandwich, making the connection between pop culture and Christian faith, or telling everyone about her ten nieces and nephews.

connect with Melissa

 MelissaZaldivar.com    @MelissaZaldivar

Dear Reader,

Thank you for selecting a Revell book! We're so happy to be part of your life through this work.

Revell's mission is to publish books that offer hope and help for meeting life's challenges, and that bring comfort and inspiration. We know that the right words at the right time can make all the difference; it is our goal with every title to provide just the words you need.

We believe in building lasting relationships with readers, and we'd love to get to know you better. If you have any feedback, questions, or just want to chat about your experience reading this book, please email us directly at publisher@revellbooks.com. Your insights are incredibly important to us, and it would be our pleasure to hear how we can better serve you.

We look forward to hearing from you and having the chance to enhance your experience with Revell Books.

The Publishing Team at Revell Books
A Division of Baker Publishing Group
publisher@revellbooks.com

Revell